Learning Through Literature

GRADES 2-3

*written by Diane Badden, Mary Anne Haffner,
Sue Ireland, Sarah J. McCutcheon, and Kathy Wolf*

edited by Diane Badden, Lynn Bemer, and Kathy Wolf

*illustrated by Pam Hall Crane, Susan Hodnett,
Rebecca Saunders, Barry Slate,
and Jennifer Tipton*

cover design by Pam Hall Crane

TABLE OF CONTENTS

Why Should I Use Literature As A Teaching Tool?

Because it works. Research shows that reading "real books" is the best way to learn to read, speak, and listen. Children who are exposed to good literature are students who learn to speak, listen, write, and read with confidence—and pleasure! Reading from children's books also gives students an opportunity to practice the reading skills they've been taught. It helps to develop vocabularies, provides a model for writing, strengthens listening skills, and exposes children to richer language than that often found in basals with controlled vocabularies.

Most of all, literature helps to foster a joy in reading and a hunger for books that will last a lifetime. Bringing "real books" into your classroom as a teaching tool is a challenge well worth taking.

How Can I Get Started?

First, you don't have to throw away your basals in order to use literature in your classroom! You can begin slowly, gradually adding more literature-based activities to your instruction. Try the following tips for getting started and those listed on page 3:

One of the simplest ways to begin a literature program is to read daily to your students. Follow up each day's reading with a discussion about characters, plot, dialogue, favorite parts, etc. Introduce new vocabulary. Involve the students in exploring the book further using the creative extension activities and reproducibles included in this book.

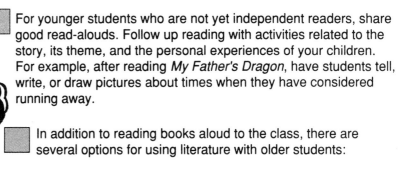

For younger students who are not yet independent readers, share good read-alouds. Follow up reading with activities related to the story, its theme, and the personal experiences of your children. For example, after reading *My Father's Dragon*, have students tell, write, or draw pictures about times when they have considered running away.

In addition to reading books aloud to the class, there are several options for using literature with older students:

1. Choose a book to use with your entire class (one copy per child).
2. Divide students into groups according to ability or interests. Choose an appropriate book for each group to read (approximately ten copies per group). In order to discuss the book so that everyone is involved, meet with small groups of students while the rest of the class is reading.
3. Pair up students of similar abilities or interests. Help each pair of "reading buddies" select a book to read together. Buddies can discuss their book, write individual reactions to and thoughts about the book in journals, and help each other with difficult vocabulary.

To obtain multiple copies, select books that are available in less expensive paperback editions.

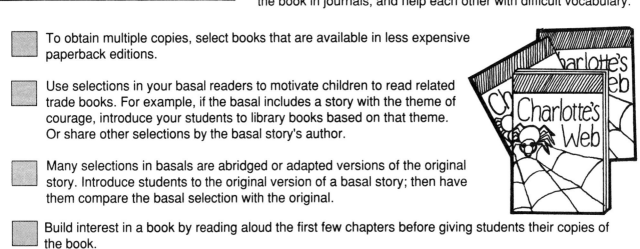

Use selections in your basal readers to motivate children to read related trade books. For example, if the basal includes a story with the theme of courage, introduce your students to library books based on that theme. Or share other selections by the basal story's author.

Many selections in basals are abridged or adapted versions of the original story. Introduce students to the original version of a basal story; then have them compare the basal selection with the original.

Build interest in a book by reading aloud the first few chapters before giving students their copies of the book.

Tips For Using Literature As A Teaching Tool

- Be excited about reading! Talk with students about what you are reading. Let them see you reading whenever possible. Model the kind of reading behavior you desire to see in your students.

- Educate yourself about what good literature is and isn't. Teachers need to read what they recommend, so become a reader of children's books. Ask your media specialist to help you choose quality books to read and share with your students.

- Read aloud to your class every day.

- Studies show that students don't read much during their free time. Provide time daily for students to read in your classroom. Be sure to schedule a specific time for silent reading, not just relegating it to something to be done when seatwork has been completed.

- Fill your classroom library with a variety of books—folklore, myths, tall tales, nonfiction, biographies, picture books, realistic fiction, etc.—on a wide variety of topics. Include other reading material such as newspapers, magazines, and brochures.

- Give students many opportunities to respond to what they're reading through book talks, informal discussions, letters, artwork, etc.

- Listen to your students' recommendations. Ask regularly, "Have you read a good book lately?"

- Relate reading to your writing instruction. For example, if students are to write riddles, feature examples of good riddle books before writing begins.

- Give students opportunities to explore literature in depth. Study a particular genre or the work of a certain author or illustrator.

- Place books that are read aloud in the classroom reading collection so that children can reread familiar books.

- Tape-record books that you read aloud. Have the cassette available (with a copy of the book) at a listening center.

- Invite volunteers, such as senior citizens, parents, or older students, into the classroom to read with individual children.

- Have students keep reading journals or diaries in which they write their reactions to books they're reading.

- Invite students to talk about books they've read. Let children present live "book commercials" during which they try to "sell" their books to the class.

- Keep a file box and index cards at a reading center. When a child finishes a book, let him fill out a card with the book's title and author, two to three sentences about the book (without giving away the plot), and his evaluation of the book. When a student is looking for a good book to read, all he has to do is look in the file box.

Strega Nona

retold and illustrated by Tomie dePaola

Strega Nona is an old Italian folktale that teaches a lesson about greediness. When Grandma Witch sings to her magic pasta pot, it boils up some pasta "nice and hot." Unfortunately, when the pot gets into the hands of an inquisitive boy named Big Anthony, the whole town is threatened by an avalanche of pasta!

The Author

Tomie dePaola (de-*pow*-la) is among the most prolific authors of self-illustrated children's books. He says he made the decision to become an artist and author of books when he was four. After graduating from Pratt Institute in 1956, dePaola spent six months in a Benedictine monastery where he says he was "sort of the resident artist." About his art style, dePaola says, "…I'm drawn to Romanesque and folk art. I think that my style is very close to those—very simple and direct. I simplify." Tomie dePaola says his dream is to have one of his books touch some individual child and change that child's life for the better.

Extension Activities

• This story takes place long ago in the Italian province of Calabria. Have students locate Ital on a map of Europe. Direct them to the toe of the boot where they will find Calabria. Read passages from the story and ask children to infer the meaning of *grazia* and *si*.

• Boil a pot of pasta! Cook up several kinds of pasta and serve them with spaghetti sauce. Or have children help you prepare a favorite Italian pasta dish. Fettuccine, anyone?

• Make a pasta picture. Provide students with different pasta noodles and shapes such as bows, shells, wheels, and elbow macaroni. Have students draw a scene from the story on construction paper and paste pasta on the design.

• Read *The Sorcerer's Apprentice* aloud to the class or show the Disney video version. Have childre compare this version to the dilemm in *Strega Nona*. Read and discuss other stories in which magic and greediness played a part including:
 Sylvester And The Magic Pebble by William Steig
 Jack And The Beanstalk
 The Magic Porridge Pot by Paul Galdone

Creative Writing Activities

People came to Strega Nona to cure headaches and warts. She also made special potions for girls who wanted husbands. Ask each student to think of a problem he would like to cure. Have students write their magic potions or chants on recipe cards.

Strega Nona needed someone to help her tend her house and garden, so she put up a sign in the town square. Perhaps today she would have placed an ad in the local newspaper. Have each student create a help-wanted ad for Strega Nona. What skills would a witch's assistant need? Post the ads on a bulletin board for all to read.

Have each student choose an ad, other than his own, and write a story telling what happened when he got the job as Strega Nona's helper. What would it be like to work for Grandma Witch? Write the following story starter on the board if you wish to stimulate imaginations: "I knew I was in trouble the first day on my new job. My employer was a strange old lady who kept a pet goat in the house and talked to a pot.... "

Ask each student to draw a picture and write a newspaper article for this headline: "Town Threatened By Pasta Flood!" Decorate stories with macaroni, shells, bows, and wheels.

Demonstrate how noodles are made with a pasta machine. The word pasta means "dough" in Italian. Have students write paragraphs describing ravioli, lasagna, spaghetti, or another pasta dish.

Critical Thinking Questions

1. Why do you think people talked about Strega Nona in whispers?

2. Why do you think Big Anthony disobeyed Strega Nona?

3. How did Big Anthony feel when the townspeople thought he was lying about the magic pot? If you were Big Anthony, how would you have responded to the townspeople?

4. If you had a magic pot, what food would it give you? How would you use the food?

5. What might have happened if Big Anthony had known how to stop the pot?

6. Do you think the punishment fit the crime in this story? Why or why not? What might be another punishment for Anthony's greediness?

7. What would you have done to stop the flood of pasta?

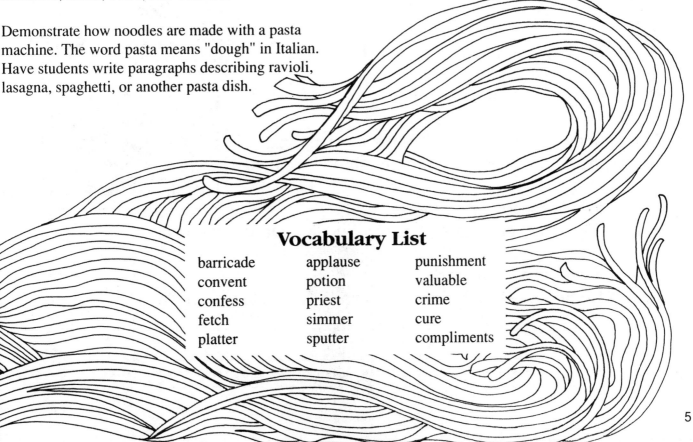

Vocabulary List

barricade	applause	punishment
convent	potion	valuable
confess	priest	crime
fetch	simmer	cure
platter	sputter	compliments

Six Steps To Perfect Pasta

Number these steps in order to make perfect pasta.

_____ Add pasta to boiling water and return to boil.

_____ Fill a large pot with four quarts of water.

_____ Add one tablespoon of salt to water and bring to a rapid boil.

_____ Cook uncovered for 12–16 minutes, stirring occasionally.

_____ Serve with your favorite sauce.

_____ Test for doneness and drain pasta.

Read each sentence pair.
Circle the sentence that tells what happened first in the story.

1. Strega Nona put up a sign in the town square.
   Big Anthony went to work for Strega Nona.

2. Strega Nona blew three kisses to the magic pot.
   Strega Nona sang to the pasta pot.

3. Big Anthony shouted for everyone to bring their forks, plates, platters and bowls.
   Big Anthony sang to the pasta pot.

4. Big Anthony filled plates for all of the townspeople.
   Some people came back for two and three helpings.

5. The people barricaded the streets.
   Big Anthony grabbed a cover and put it on the pot and sat on it.

6. Big Anthony got a tummy ache.
   Strega Nona gave Big Anthony a fork and told him to start eating.

Bonus Box: On the back, draw a picture for each circled sentence.

Pasta Pots

Read each question.
If the answer is yes, color the pot yellow.
If the answer is no, color the pot red.
Use a dictionary.

Can a dog <u>fetch</u> the newspaper?

Is a gold coin <u>valuable</u>?

Can a pot of soup <u>simmer</u>?

Can a lawn mower <u>sputter</u>?

Would a nun live in a <u>convent</u>?

Would you be telling the truth if you <u>confessed</u>?

Is there a <u>cure</u> for old age?

Would a <u>barricade</u> block traffic?

Is a <u>platter</u> a loud noise?

Do clowns like <u>applause</u>?

Is a <u>punishment</u> usually enjoyable?

Is stealing a <u>crime</u>?

Could a <u>priest</u> say prayers?

Could you drink a <u>potion</u>?

Do most people hate <u>compliments</u>?

The Punishment Must Fit The Crime

Read each sentence on the left.
Find the reason why on the right.
Draw lines to match.

Strega Nona needed someone •
to help her.

• The people did not believe Big
  Anthony's story.

Girls who wanted husbands •
went to Strega Nona.

• Big Anthony had a chance to
  make the pot cook.

Big Anthony was angry. •

• Big Anthony did not blow three kisses.

Big Anthony was glad when •
Strega Nona went out of town.

• Strega Nona made magic potions.

The pasta pot would not stop. •

• Strega Nona was getting old.

Big Anthony took a bow to the •
applause of the crowd.

• They hoped God would stop the
  flood.

The men shouted, "String •
him up!"

• They wanted to punish poor Big
  Anthony.

People barricaded the streets. •

• Big Anthony was a hero.

The priest and the sisters of •
the convent began to pray.

• The punishment fit the crime.

Anthony had a tummy ache. •

• The pasta flood was coming.

Name _____

There's A Lesson To Be Learned!

Read each sentence.
If it is a fact, color the pasta red.
If it is an opinion, color the pasta green.

1. The people in town talked about Strega Nona in whispers.

2. Big Anthony did not pay attention.

3. The pasta overflowed into the streets.

4. The townspeople should forgive poor Big Anthony.

5. Big Anthony wanted to show the townspeople that he was important.

6. The townspeople thought Strega Nona had a magic touch.

7. Big Anthony's punishment fit the crime.

8. Strega Nona should not have gone out of town.

9. The townspeople wanted to hang Big Anthony.

10. In the wrong hands, the pasta pot was dangerous.

11. The sisters of the convent should have prayed harder.

12. Greedy people want too much of a good thing.

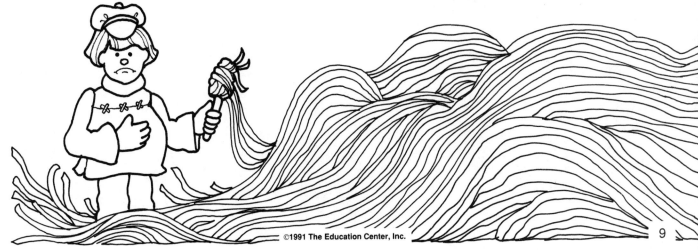

9

Sylvester And The Magic Pebble

written and illustrated by William Steig

Sylvester, the donkey, discovers that owning a magic pebble has its dangers when he accidentally turns himself into a rock! Sylvester's parents search for their beloved son to no avail. One year later, a chance picnic on Strawberry Hill reunites them. The family is so happy to have each other again that they put the pebble away in a safe. After all, what more could they wish for?

The Author

William Steig was born into an artistic family in New York City on November 14, 1907. In 1930, he started a successful career as a cartoonist. He began his second profession in 1968 when he published his first children's book, *Roland The Minstrel Pig*. He was 61 years old. *Sylvester And The Magic Pebble* followed in 1969.

Steig says each of his children's books but one began as a visual image without a theme. He explains that "…I just ramble around and discover for myself what will happen next." The author has won many awards including Caldecott Medals in 1970 for *Sylvester And The Magic Pebble* and in 1977 for *The Amazing Bone*.

Extension Activities

- Sylvester's hobby was collecting unusual pebbles. Invite a rock collector to share his collection with your class. Discuss how rocks can be categorized by color, hardness, and origin. Provide samples for students to sort by color, size, or hardness. Have each student look for an unusual pebble to share with the class. Display the rocks with the book and the title "Sylvester's Magic Pebbles."

- Read aloud one or more books that deal with magic:
  King Midas And The Golden Touch by Kathryn Hewitt (Harcourt, 1987)
  The Chocolate Touch by Patrick Skene Catling (Morrow, 1979)
  Strega Nona by Tomie dePaola (Simon & Schuster 1975)
  Jack And The Beanstalk by Laurinda Bryan Cauley (Putnam, 1983)
  Discuss how the magic powers caused trouble in each case.

- Pack a picnic basket for an imaginary picnic on Strawberry Hill! Mrs. Duncan packed alfalfa sandwiches, pickled oats, sassafras salad, and timothy compote—perfect fare for donkeys. Have students think of other foods made from oats or corn that the donkeys might take on a picnic. Make cornbread muffins or oatmeal cookies. Pack them in a picnic basket and take the class outside for a picnic on the school grounds.

Vocabulary List

hobbies	collecting
extraordinary	remarkable
ceased	vanished
gratified	startled
panicked	perplexed
bewildered	muttered
eventually	frantic
soothe	inquiring
insisted	aimlessly

...ative Writing Activities

...r. Duncan put the magic pebble in an iron safe for ...fe keeping. Place a "magic pebble" in a small, ...etal safe or lock box with a key. Place the safe at ...writing center. Instruct students to open the safe, ...ke out the pebble, make a wish, and complete this ...ory starter: This was my lucky day. I wished ...r…

...ave students draw missing donkey posters to help ...the search for Sylvester. Children should include ...formation that tells when Sylvester disappeared, ...hat he looks like, and what is offered as the ...ward.

...ave students write newspaper stories for this ...eadline: "Missing Donkey Found Alive After One ...ear As A Rock!"

...ake a collection of good luck charms: a rabbit's ...ot, a four-leaf clover, a lucky horseshoe, a lucky ...umber, a new penny, a mustard seed, and a quartz ...ystal are but a few. Have each child choose a ...ood luck charm and write a paragraph explaining ...ow it will bring good luck.

...itical Thinking Questions

Why do you think Sylvester panicked at the sight of the lion?

What do you think Sylvester should have wished for when the hungry lion appeared?

How would your parents feel if you did not come home one day?

What might have happened if Sylvester had not turned into a rock?

Why do you think Sylvester's parents locked the magic pebble away in a safe?

If you had a magic pebble, what would you wish for and why?

Magic Pebbles

Find a **synonym** from the list for the underlined
 word or words.
Draw a line to each magic pebble.

1. Sylvester found an <u>extraordinary</u> pebble.

2. The rain <u>stopped</u> suddenly and the sun came out.

3. Sylvester had never had a wish <u>filled</u> so quickly.

4. On the way home, Sylvester was <u>frightened</u> by
    a mean, hungry lion.

5. Sylvester <u>disappeared</u> without a trace.

6. The lion was <u>bewildered</u> to find a rock
    instead of a donkey.

7. <u>By and by,</u> Sylvester realized that he would be a rock
    until someone found the magic pebble.

8. They went about <u>inquiring of</u> all the neighbors.

9. The Duncans <u>wished with all their hearts</u>
    for their dear son.

10. Mr. Duncan did his best to <u>calm</u> his wife.

11. Their lives became miserable and <u>without purpose.</u>

12. When Sylvester turned back into a donkey,
    the whole family <u>hugged</u> each other.

ceased

eventually

vanished

remarkable

gratified

perplexed

aimless

startled

soothe

longed

embraced

questioning

Bonus Box: Color the pebbles beside verbs red.

Make A Wish

Help Sylvester number the sentences in each group
 to show the order in which they happened.

One rainy Saturday during vacation

_____ Sylvester wished it would stop raining.

_____ Sylvester found a shiny red pebble.

_____ Sylvester was startled by a hungry lion.

_____ Sylvester said, "I wish I were a rock."

Meanwhile back at home,

_____ Mr. and Mrs. Duncan paced the floor.

_____ At dawn, the Duncans inquired of all the neighbors.

_____ Sylvester's parents went to the police.

_____ After a month, Sylvester's parents concluded that
         something dreadful must have happened.

One day in May,

_____ Mr. and Mrs. Duncan went to Strawberry Hill for a picnic.

_____ Sylvester wished to be himself again.

_____ Mrs. Duncan sat down on a rock.

_____ Mr. Duncan found the magic pebble and put it on the rock.

Bonus Box: On the back, write what you would wish for if you had a magic pebble.

Sylvester's Problem

Blacken the correct dot.

1. Sylvester believed that the pebble was magic because
   ○ the rain ceased when he wished it.   ○ it was flaming red.

2. Sylvester wished to be a rock because
   ○ he wanted to escape from the lion.   ○ he wanted to turn to stone.

3. Sylvester could not wish himself back to normal because
   ○ he forgot the magic words.   ○ he had to be touching the pebble.

4. Sylvester's parents paced the floor because
   ○ they were angry.   ○ they were frantic with worry.

5. The dogs couldn't tell that the rock on Strawberry Hill was Sylvester because
   ○ they didn't sniff the right rock.   ○ it didn't have the donkey's scent.

6. The Duncans thought that they would never see their son again because
   ○ something dreadful had happened.   ○ Sylvester had run away.

7. Sylvester felt hopeless and unhappy because
   ○ he felt he would be a rock forever.   ○ he was cold.

8. Mr. Duncan insisted that his wife go with him on a picnic because
   ○ he knew Sylvester would be there.   ○ he wanted them to be happy.

9. Sylvester awoke from his deep winter sleep because
   ○ the sun warmed him up.   ○ his mother sat on him.

10. Mr. Duncan put the magic pebble in an iron safe because
    ○ they couldn't wish for anything more.   ○ it was dangerous.

My Life As A Rock

Think of a new ending for Sylvester's story.
Finish the story.

    I realized I might be a rock forever and I tried to get used to it.
As the seasons passed, I watched and waited for someone to
find the magic pebble beside me. _____

_____

_____

_____

_____

Draw Sylvester as a rock.
Draw the magic pebble beside him.
Draw what he saw around him.

Big Bad Bruce

by Bill Peet

Bruce is a big, brown bear and the resident bully of Forevergreen Forest. Bruce's idea of fun is scaring the wits out of everyone. All the forest animals run for their lives when Bruce is feeling frisky. The tables are turned on Bruce however, when he tries to play tricks on Roxy the Witch and her cat Klinker. Roxy cooks up a magical blueberry pie to teach Bruce a lesson. After Bruce gobbles up the pie, he discovers that he has shrunk! He's no longer so big or so bad. Roxy comes to his rescue and decides to keep the little bear.

The Author

Born January 29, 1915, to Orion and Thelma Hopkins, Bill Peet's surname was changed in 1947. In his childhood years, Saturdays and summers were set aside for exploring creeks and wooded areas outskirting Indianapolis. As a boy, Bill Peet had an interest in animals; he longed to see and learn more about them. His first trip to the Cincinnati zoo taught him a valuable lesson. He had bought film earlier with the money he earned during the summer. He wanted to photograph each zoo animal. The day was perfect for taking photographs, but the shutter on his camera was not working correctly. The film he had spent his hard-earned money on was ruined! Bill Peet learned to rely on his artistic talents, and from that day on he carried a sketch pad and pencil wherever he went.

Bill Peet started his career illustrating greeting cards. He regards drawing as his main hobby, which started when he was old enough to hold a crayon in his hand! It wasn't until 1959, at the age of 44, that Bill Peet published his first children's book. Since then he has written many more and has received awards. His stories are enjoyed by children throughout the world. Among his books are: *The Pinkish, Purplish, Bluish Egg; Ella; Hubert's Hair-Raising Adventure; Huge Harold; Randy's Dandy Lions; Smokey;* and *Chester.*

Vocabulary

brute	raucous	diminishing	haunches
blunder	lummox	gape	desperation
aspens	smithereens	bewildered	runt
canyons	frantic	recognized	pell-mell
grubs	smidgeon	brambles	snuffling
bluff	cackled	thrashing	drowsy
crafty	lumbered	bedraggled	scruff
heave	dwindled	jittery	aroma
vicious			

Extension Activities

- Allow students to make predictions by first reading the story aloud. Stop on page 7 and ask, "What do you think the awful mistake is?" Stop on page 20 and ask, "What will happen to Bruce after eating the magical pie?" Stop on page 30 and say, "What will happen next?" Compare students' predictions with what actually happened.

- Give students ABC order practice with blueberry pie words. Label construction paper, pie-shaped cutouts with vocabulary words from the story. Store these in an aluminum pie plate at a center. Students place the shapes in alphabetical order and check the answer key on the bottom of the pie plate.

- Bruce is a bully in the beginning of the story. Ask your students what makes a bully act mean. As a group, brainstorm ways to discourage bullies.

After reading the story, have students find out about real bears. Working individually or in groups, have students use encyclopedias, magazines, and library books to answer questions about these large mammals. Write information on paper paws and display with the title "The Bear Facts." For a special follow-up, show *The Bear,* an RCA home video that is 92 minutes long.

Celebrate the end of the story in a delicious way. Have students create a magical, no-cook berry dessert. For every eight children, you will need:

     1 package (3 oz.) blackberry gelatin
     2/3 cup boiling water
     2 cups ice cubes
     1 container (8 oz.) nondairy whipped cream
     1 cup fresh blueberries
     1 package of 8 graham cracker tart shells

    Dissolve gelatin in boiling water. Add ice cubes. Stir constantly until gelatin is thickened, about 2–3 minutes.

    Remove any unmelted ice cubes. Blend in whipped cream with a wire whisk. Whip until smooth. Fold in fruit.

    Chill if necessary until mixture will mound. Spoon into small tart shells. Chill 3 hours.

Creative Writing Activities

Reread the ingredients in Roxy's recipe for her magic blueberry pie on page 14. Ask students to create their own magical mixtures for curing a bully or making someone tiny. Or have students create a disappearing spell, a growth potion, a smart pill, or a kindness concoction. Give each child half of a file folder to simulate a giant recipe card. Students decorate cards, add their recipes, and post them on a bulletin board with the title "Cooking Up Some Magic!"

The animals of Forevergreen Forest owe a debt of gratitude to Roxy for ridding them of Big Bad Bruce. Have students pretend they are grateful forest inhabitants. Have them write thank-you notes to the crafty witch and sign the notes with animal names.

Bruce had shrunk to the size of a chipmunk. Ask children to imagine how their lives would change if they were that small. Have them complete this story starter: I drank from the bottle and fell into a deep sleep. When I awakened, everything looked huge! I had shrunk to the size of a....

The story ends with tiny Bruce up to his old bullying ways. Now he's intimidating the grasshoppers, beetles, and caterpillars. Challenge students to come up with a way for the bugs to solve their problems with Bruce. Have each student write and illustrate his solution. Share the creative solutions with the class.

Critical Thinking Questions

1. How does Bruce's behavior change after he eats the magic pie? In what ways does it stay the same?

2. What might have happened if Roxy's recipe had not worked? What could the animals have done to solve their problem with Bruce?

3. Roxy could have said, "She who laughs last, laughs best." What does this saying mean? Do you agree or disagree with it, and why?

4. If Bruce wanted to come back to live in Forevergreen Forest, what rules do you think he should have to follow?

5. For Bruce the most fun was rock tumbling. What could he have done for fun instead of throwing rocks?

Prizewinning Pies

Here are some prizewinning words.

Read each word.
Color the ribbon.
Use the code.

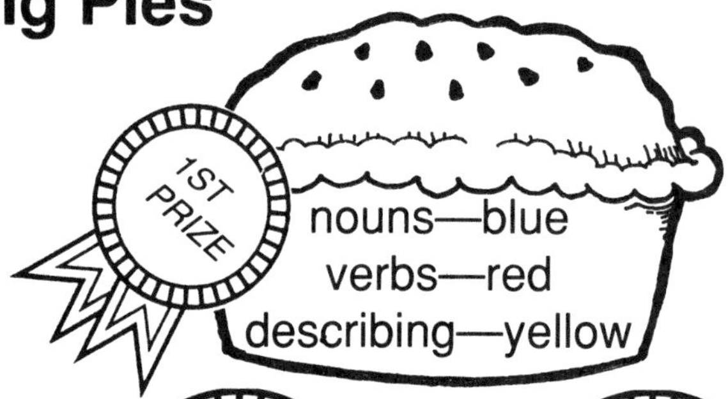

1ST PRIZE

nouns—blue
verbs—red
describing—yellow

shrieked	magical	runt	aroma
canyons	scurry	drowsy	jittery
crafty	heaved	brambles	lummox
	grubs	rambled	lumbered

Bonus Box: Make a list of foods made with blueberries.

©1991 The Education Center, Inc.

Name _____

Bruce On The Loose

Read each sentence.
If it could happen in real life, color the bear.

 1. Bruce was a shaggy brute of a bear.

 2. The bear ate a blueberry pie.

 3. Bruce found himself nose to beak with a giant quail.

 4. The huge boulder smashed pine trees and aspens.

 5. Roxy put a magic spell on the blueberry pie.

 6. Bruce ate beetles and grubs.

 7. As Bruce slept he gradually grew smaller and smaller.

 8. The bear exploded into great fits of laughter.

 9. Roxy was out picking blueberries with her cat.

 10. Bruce flopped down next to a tree to take a rest.

 11. The tiny bear threw pebbles to scare the bugs.

 12. Bruce smelled the aroma of blueberries and honey.

 13. The cat and the bear ate out of the same bowl.

 14. Roxy loved flowers, birds, and animals.

 15. Klinker carried Bruce by the scruff of the neck.

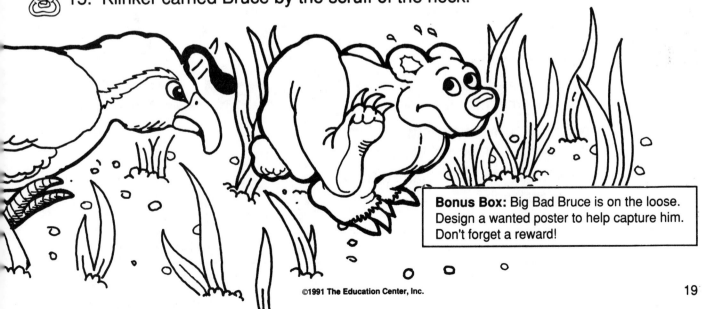

Bonus Box: Big Bad Bruce is on the loose. Design a wanted poster to help capture him. Don't forget a reward!

19

Prowl For Pronouns

A **pronoun** is a word that takes the place of a noun.

Example:
<u>Bruce</u> ran through the forest.
He was tired.

He stands for *Bruce.*

Read each pair of sentences. Look at the <u>underlined</u> <u>pronoun</u>. Circle the noun that the pronoun stands for.

1. Bruce tumbled the rocks.
<u>They</u> smashed the trees.

2. Bruce found a big boulder.
He gave <u>it</u> a mighty heave.

3. The animals kept a sharp eye on Bruce.
Just in case <u>he</u> gave them any trouble.

4. Bruce found a log.
He found grubs and beetles under <u>it</u>.

5. Roxy and Klinker charged up the hill.
"That rock could have smashed <u>us</u> to smithereens!'

6. The clever witch made a blueberry pie.
<u>She</u> added a diminishing spell to it.

7. There was no sign of Bruce in the forest.
But Roxy could hear <u>him</u> snorting around.

8. "Grrowf yourself!" the witch said to the bear.
"<u>You</u> don't scare me."

9. The drowsy Bruce sat down next to a tree.
<u>He</u> fell asleep by it.

10. Roxy and her cat made a plan.
"<u>We</u> will show that bear," she said.

11. The witch grew fond of the tiny bear.
She decided to keep <u>him</u> that way.

12. She picked out a pine stump.
Then Roxy put the pie on <u>it</u>.

13. Klinker the cat liked the bear.
<u>They</u> slept in the corner near the stove.

14. There were lots of rocks in Forevergreen Forest.
Bruce could find great jumbles of <u>them</u>.

15. Laugh while you can, Mr. Bear," warned Roxy.
"<u>I</u> will have the last laugh."

Bonus Box: Find nine more pronouns above. Draw a box around each of them.

Name _____

What A Jumble!

Help tell the story of *Big Bad Bruce*.
Read each sentence.
Cut and paste the sentences in order below.

The crafty witch hatched a plan.	
Bruce rolled a boulder that just missed Roxy.	
Bruce gobbled up the magical blueberry pie.	
Bruce flipped pebbles at the bugs in the garden.	
The forest animals chased the small bear.	
As Bruce slept he grew smaller and smaller.	
Bruce tumbled rocks to scare the animals.	
The old witch took Bruce home to live with her.	

Bonus Box: What part did you like best in *Big Bad Bruce?* Draw and color a picture of your favorite part.

Amelia Bedelia

by Peggy Parish

Jim Trelease, author of *The Read-Aloud Handbook*, calls Amelia Bedelia "America's most lovable maid…." Her adventures have tickle children for almost 30 years. Amelia Bedelia's first day at work is a disaster when she insists on taking directions literally. She *draws* th drapes, *dusts* the furniture, *changes* the towels, *dresses* the chicke and *trims* the meat in very unusual ways. Mr. and Mrs. Rogers are about to fire Amelia when they taste her superb lemon-meringue p

The Author

Peggy Parish was born and raised in Manning, South Carolina, where she now resides. After teaching third grade for many years, she decided to write books for children. Since 1962, Ms. Parish has written more than 30 books. Her Amelia Bedelia series has been popular with primary children since the first book was published in 1963. Ms. Parish says, "Children have always been in my life, so writing stories for children came naturally…. I don't try to teach anything in my stories—I write just for fun."

Vocabulary

folks	scissors	snip	furniture
container	icebox	powder	aired
exclaim	measure	lemon-meringue	fade
pinch	oven	switched	drapes

Extension Activities

- After reading Amelia Bedelia, serve lemon-meringue pie or have students make individual lemon pies! For an individual pie, place two graham crackers in a Ziploc bag. Carefully seal the bag before crushing the crackers. Add one teaspoon each of sugar and softened butter to the cracker crumbs; then reseal the bag and mix the ingredients together. Spoon the cracker mixture into the bottom of an aluminum tart pan or paper cup. In a tightly sealed baby food jar, shake together one tablespoon of instant lemon pudding and 1/4 cup of milk. Pour the thickened pudding atop the crust.

- Ask students to describe Amelia Bedelia's unusual hat. Have each student create a new hat to replace Amelia Bedelia's old one. Provide materials such a paper plates, tissue paper, and ribbon, lace, or fabric scraps. Students may wish to wear their creations in an Amelia Bedelia fashion show.

- Have groups of students dramatize scenes from the story in a cooperative learning activity. Have each group create props and costumes to perform one scene. Props may include dusting powder, tattered towels, a drawing of drapes, a dressed chicken, light bulbs on a clothesline, and a lemon-meringue pie.

Discuss words that have double meanings and idiomatic expressions. Have each student write an idiomatic expression from the list and illustrate it for a bulletin board entitled "Raining Cats And Dogs."

   raining cats and dogs
   full of bologna
   in a pickle
   all thumbs
   hit the roof

Read other books about Amelia Bedelia including:
   Amelia Bedelia And The Surprise Shower
   Amelia Bedelia And The Baby
   Amelia Bedelia Goes Camping
   Play Ball, Amelia Bedelia
   Amelia Bedelia's Family Album
Have each student choose a favorite scene from one of these stories to share with the class by creating a shoe box diorama.

Ask students to bring in contributions for an Amelia Bedelia Museum. Artifacts in this museum collection represent articles from any of the Amelia Bedelia stories. Have each student write the name of the book and a description of his article on an index card. Place the index cards beside the objects on display tables in the hall.

What would a radio broadcast or TV talk show with Amelia Bedelia and Mr. and Mrs. Rogers sound like? Choose students to play the roles of the book characters and a famous talk show host or hostess. Have the class brainstorm questions for the host to ask each guest.
  Examples:
  Amelia, what is it like to work for the richest
   people in town?
  Mr. Rogers, why did you decide to keep Amelia
   on?
Tape-record the interview and play it back for the class for some chuckles.

Creative Writing Activities

With your class, discuss what a maid does. Find want ads for domestic help in the newspaper. Have each student write a want ad for a maid to help him or her with chores. Cover a bulletin board with newspaper. Post the ads on the bulletin board with the title "Help Wanted."

- Ask students to imagine how Amelia Bedelia might complete one of the tasks from this list. Have students write and illustrate their stories.
   feed the fish
   change the baby
   change the sheets
   take out the trash
   write a letter
   make a sponge cake
   pot the plants

- Have students think of tasks they would like a maid to do for them. Have each child make a list of jobs for his own personal maid.

- Have each student write a letter to Amelia Bedelia asking for her famous lemon-meringue pie recipe.

Critical Thinking Questions

1. Do you think Amelia Bedelia was a good maid? Why or why not?

2. What might happen if Amelia came to work for your family?

3. How do you think Amelia felt about the mistakes she made?

4. How could Mr. and Mrs. Rogers help Amelia to not make mistakes?

5. Why did Mr. and Mrs. Rogers decide to keep Amelia as their maid? What would you have done?

6. What is one thing you learned about following directions from this story?

Lemon-Meringue Surprise

Read each sentence.
Decide whether it is fact or opinion.
Circle the letter in the correct column.

		Fact	Opinion
1.	Mrs. Rogers should have fired Amelia Bedelia.	R	W
2.	Mr. Rogers loved Amelia's lemon-meringue pie.	I	O
3.	Amelia Bedelia drew the drapes.	H	G
4.	Mrs. Rogers should not have left Amelia home alone on her first day on the job.	A	I
5.	The chicken was dressed in pants.	G	P
6.	Amelia Bedelia's hat was ugly.	U	E
7.	Mrs. Rogers was madder than she had ever been.	R	T
8.	Mr. and Mrs. Rogers decided that Amelia must stay.	S	Y
9.	Mr. and Mrs. Rogers lived in a grand house.	G	B
10.	Mr. and Mrs. Rogers were the nicest folks in town.	J	E
11.	Amelia Bedelia was a good maid.	V	S
12.	Amelia tried to do exactly what was written on the list.	X	M

**What was in Amelia Bedelia's recipe for lemon-meringue pie?
To find out, write the circled letters in the blanks below.**

___ ___ ___   ___ ___ ___   ___ ___ ___ ___ ___ ___
 8   4 12   6   9   5   1   3   2   7 10 11

Name _____

Amelia Bedelia Is Puzzled

Read each sentence below.
Fill in the blanks.
Use the word bank.
Write the words in the puzzle.

Across

1. Amelia Bedelia made a _____-meringue pie.
2. Amelia dusted the furniture with _____.
3. A refrigerator is also called an _____.
4. Amelia put the pie in the _____.
5. Mrs. Rogers did not want the furniture to _____.
6. Amelia Bedelia used scissors to _____ the towels.

Down

1. Amelia lifted the _____ of the box.
2. Amelia put a little of this and a _____ of that into a bowl.
7. The lemon pie had a fluffy _____ topping.
8. Amelia found a _____ box to put the chicken in.
9. Mr. and Mrs. Rogers were rich _____.
10. Amelia put the lights out to _____ them.

Word Bank

lemon	icebox	folks	pinch	powder	snip
air	nice	meringue	fade	lid	oven

Name _____

Jobs For Amelia Bedelia

Pretend that Amelia Bedelia is your maid.
Remember: Amelia does exactly what she is told.
Tell Amelia how to complete these jobs.
Write the steps in order.

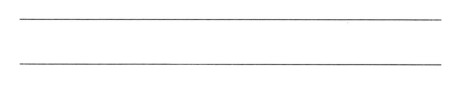

1. Take out the trash.

_____

_____

_____

2. Change the sheets.

_____

_____

_____

3. Clean under the bed.

_____

4. Dust the furniture.

_____

_____

_____

26   ©1991 The Education Center, Inc.

Name _____

Now That Takes The Cake!

An *idiom* has a meaning that does not come from the actual words.
Example: It's raining cats and dogs.

Some words have *double meanings*.
Example: *draw* a picture and *draw* the drapes.

Cut out and match the meanings to the pies.
Put a dot of glue at each dot to glue pies.
Choose one sentence to illustrate on the back.

It's raining cats and dogs.

It's time to hit the sack.

The good news put him on top of the world.

The thief was in a pickle when the cops arrived.

Draw the drapes.

Bob is feeling under the weather today.

Mary has a green thumb.

When Mrs. Rogers saw her tattered towels, she hit the roof!

Put the lights out.

- -

It's raining very hard.

Turn off the lights.

The news made him very happy.

Mary can make plants grow.

The thief was in trouble.

She was very angry.

Close the curtains.

Bob is ill today.

It's bedtime.

The One In The Middle Is The Gree[ ] Kangaroo

by Judy Blume

For second grader Freddy Dissel, being the middle child in his family is like being a "nothing in the middle." When he gets a part in the fifth- and sixth-grade play, however, he proves to himself and others that he has special talents. Freddy's a hit on stage as th[ ] high-jumping Green Kangaroo, and he realizes that ju[ ] being himself makes him special anywhere.

The Author

Judy Blume enjoyed a happy family life. She was close to her parents but didn't feel that she could *really* talk to them. As a child, she spent much of her time in a library poring over children's books. She recalls not being able to find books that really dealt with the frustrations of growing up.

Ms. Blume draws upon these feelings when writing. Ms. Blume's characters feel, talk, and act the way she thinks a normal child of that age group would. In doing so she has broken into many areas that, when she was a child, were not accepted in children's literature. Many parents disapprove of Ms. Blume's writing but she insists she will do it her way!

Ms. Blume did not reach overnight success and for several years received rejection upon rejection. She reflects on this as being an excellent growing period in her writing career. Many agree since Ms. Blume has received many awards for her books and is thoroughly enjoyed by youngsters everywhere.

Extension Activities

• Discuss sibling birth order and how everyone's position in the family affects what is expected of him or her. Take a survey of how many children in your class are the oldest child (includes only child), the middle child, and the youngest child. Together graph the information with a bar, picture, or circle graph.

• Have students hop down to the library to locate facts about the kangaroo. Enlarge and duplicate the kangaroo pattern on page 33 for each child. Write a question from below on each kangaroo, and have[ ] children answer the questions on the backs. Store[ ] these kangaroo facts in a pocket glued to the fron[ ] of a large kangaroo cutout.

What is a group of kangaroos called? (a mob)
What is the leader of a kangaroo mob called? ([ ] boomer)
How far can a kangaroo jump? (30 feet)
How fast can a kangaroo travel? (at speeds up [ ] 35 miles per hour)
What is a flyer? (a female kangaroo)
What is a baby kangaroo called? (a joey)

• Freddy wanted to tell his family what it was like being the middle child. Have students role-play t[ ] parts of Freddy and his family members in these situations:

"Mom, wearing Mike's hand-me-downs makes[ ] me feel…. I would like a new outfit be-cause…"
"Dad, sharing a room with Mike is tough be-cause…. I would like a special place of my own because…"
"Mike, when your friends are around, I wish y[ ] would…"
"Ellen, I wish you would stop…"

• Read Judy Blume's *Freckle Juice* to the class. Compare and contrast the characters, plot, setting[ ] and problems and solutions of each book. Discus[ ] how Judy Blume writes about the problems of growing up and feeling good about oneself.

Creative Writing Activities

Freddy got rave reviews for his performance in the play. Have each student write a review for the school newspaper telling how good Freddy was as the green kangaroo. Students can include quotes from members of the audience and cast.

As a middle child, Freddy feels "like the peanut butter part of a sandwich, squeezed between Mike and Ellen." Together, brainstorm other "in-the-middle" comparisons. Have students write and illustrate their comparisons as similes such as:

  Freddy was like a sardine in the middle of the can.
  Freddy was like the cream in the middle of an Oreo cookie.
  Freddy was like a hot dog in the middle of a roll.
  Freddy was like the pages between two book covers.

Make a class book by binding the illustrations between the covers of a sandwich-shaped file folder.

Teach students how to write hink pinks. Have children think of definitions for these rhyming word pairs. For example: What do you call a happy boy? Answer: A glad lad.

smart part	green scene	gay play
proud crowd	brighter writer	neat feet
other brother	cute suit	bright light
fine line	stage rage	top hop

Have each student choose one of these opinions and write a paragraph telling why he or she agrees.

  Being the baby of the family would be the worst.
  I would not like to be an only child.
  The oldest child always has the most responsibility.

Vocabulary

Chapter 1	Chapter 2	Chapter 3
problems	special	mirror
sandwich	decided	neighbors
squeezed	mumbled	costume
pinched	auditorium	whispered
nursery	hollered	ruffled
figured	attention	stomach
	sponge	bounced
	believe	audience

Critical Thinking Questions

1. Freddy thought that being in the middle was like being a big nothing. Why do you think he felt this way? Do you agree or disagree with him?

2. If you were Mr. or Mrs. Dissel, how would you show each child in your family that he or she was special?

3. Why so you think Mike and Ellen thought Freddy's part in the play was "no big deal"?

4. In what other ways could Freddy prove to himself and his family that he was special?

5. Even though the play was put on by the fifth and sixth graders, why did Ms. Matson give Freddy a part?

6. What part of this story reminds you of your family?

7. If you could make your family proud of you in one special way, what would it be?

Springing Into Definitions

Read each sentence.
Replace the underlined part of the sentence with a word from the Word Bank.

1. Freddy <u>thought</u> he would make a great kangaroo in the play.

    _____

2. He <u>yelled</u>, "I AM FREDDY. I WANT TO BE IN THE PLAY."_____

3. Freddy's <u>clothes for the play</u> were a green kangaroo suit. _____

4. He would <u>say over and over</u> his lines in front of a mirror. _____

5. Freddy's old bedroom became a <u>room for baby</u> Ellen. _____

6. At last he <u>made up his mind</u> to try out for the part. _____

7. Some of the Dissels' <u>friends who lived nearby</u> came to the play. _____

8. Ms. Gumber <u>messed up</u> his hair before he went on stage. _____

9. It was time to face the <u>people who would watch the play</u>. _____

10. His <u>belly</u> felt uneasy. _____

11. The children knew they could not <u>speak in a soft voice</u>. _____

12. To get their attention, he <u>jumped</u> across the stage. _____

Word Bank

nursery	figured	neighbors	decided
hollered	practice	ruffled	costume
bounced	whisper	audience	stomach

Bonus Box: Freddy's success in the play calls for a celebration. Name three ways the Dissel family can celebrate.

Quite A Cast Of Characters

Read each line from the story.
Write the name of the character who said it.

Freddy	Mike	Ellen	Mr. Dissel	Mrs. Dissel

Ms. Gumber   Ms. Matson

1. She whispered, "Break a leg." _____

2. "You shouldn't be mean to Ellen….She's just a baby!" _____

3. "Get out of the way, kid." _____

4. "Hello, everyone. I am the Green Kangaroo. Welcome." _____

5. "I think it's wonderful that you got the part in the play." _____

6. "I think you will be fine as the Green Kangaroo." _____

7. "Why would they pick you? *Everybody* can jump." _____

8. "A special thank you for our second grader, Freddy Dissel." _____

9. "Guess what, everyone? Guess what I'm going to be?" _____

10. "We're all proud of you, Freddy." _____

11. "I can talk loud. Listen to this." She screamed. "See how loud I can talk."

_____

12. "I'll find out if they need any second graders to help." _____

Bonus Box: Pretend you are Mike or Ellen. Draw a cartoon of what you will say to Freddy after you see him in the play.

There's A Riddle In The Middle

If the sentence tells a true statement about the story, circle the letter in the **FACT** column.

If the sentence tells a feeling about the story, circle the letter under **OPINION**.
Then print the letter answer in the riddle below.

		FACT	OPINION
1.	The Dissel family has five people.	B	C
2.	Freddy should not have to give up his room to Ellen.	I	U
3.	"Break a leg" means "good luck."	A	O
4.	Family rules are unfair.	S	P
5.	Mike did not believe that Freddy had a part in the play.	M	R
6.	The clapping of the audience told Freddy that he had done a good job in the play.	R	H
7.	Because Ellen is the youngest child, she should be treated like the baby in the family.	E	A
8.	Freddy was nervous before the play started.	S	W
9.	Because Freddy knew what to do in the play, he should not have been nervous.	Y	O
10.	Real kangaroos are not green.	I	L
11.	A bouncing green kangaroo may be funny.	S	N
12.	Freddy was proud of his part in the play.	L	J
13.	Judy Blume is the best children's writer.	V	M

What do you call a group of 100 kangaroos?

a __ __ __ of __ __ __ __ __ __ __ __ __ __
  5 9 1   13 3 6 11 2 4 10 7 12 8

Bonus Box: Kangaroos live in groups called *mobs.* Hop over to the library to find out which animals live in *herds, schools, gaggles, pods, bands,* and *colonies.*

Kangaroo Review

How did you feel about the book?

1. Complete each sentence.
2. Color the kangaroo.
3. Cut out the kangaroo and pages.
4. Staple your book.

I felt sad for Freddy when	I was overjoyed when
I laughed when	I agree with Freddy that

©1991 The Education Center, Inc.

©1991 The Education Center, Inc.

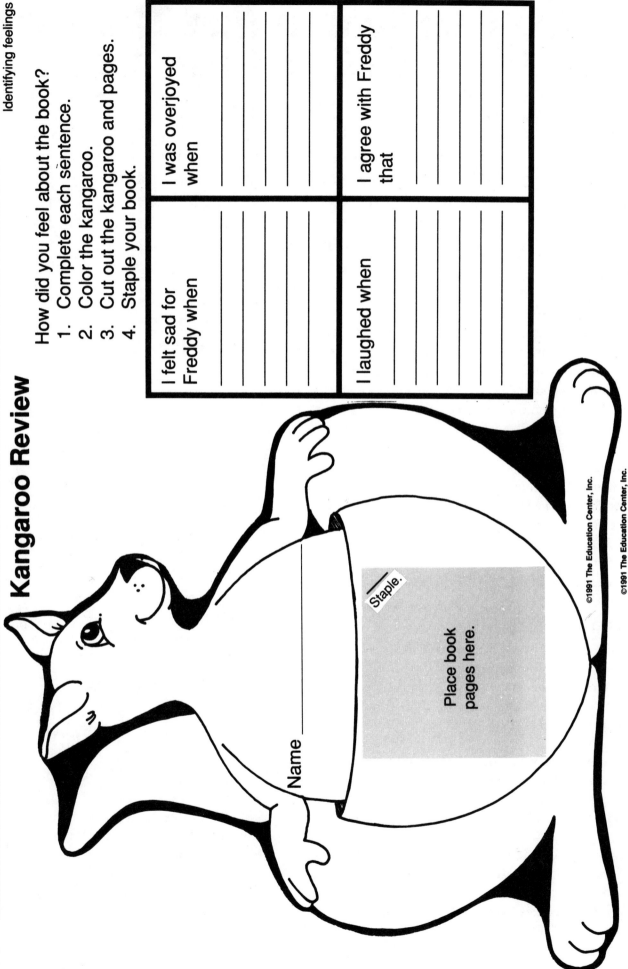

Name _____

Staple.

Place book pages here.

Note To The Teacher: Staple booklet on top right corner of pouch.

Cam Jansen And The Myster Of The Circus Clown

by David A. Adler

Being at the circus with Aunt Molly was lots of fun for Cam "The Camera" Jansen and her friend Eric. That is, until Cam zoomed in on some unauthorized funny business. In a flash, Cam and Eric are hot o the trail of two cleverly disguised pickpockets. Can Cam's photograp memory help her outsmart the criminals? Or will the pickpockets get the last laughs? This fast-paced mystery adventure will have even yo most reluctant reader reading page after page after page!

The Author

The second-oldest of six children, David A. Adler's childhood memories are of a large house filled with children, books, and two very relaxed parents. With his parents' encouragement, Adler developed interests in art, teaching, and writing. Once a professional artist and a teacher of mathematics, Adler now devotes his time to writing children's books. Well known for his Cam Jansen Mystery series and many other diversified fictional writings, he is also a talented nonfiction writer. Though he has considered writing for adults, Adler's first love is writing for children. And what would David say is his greatest pleasure as a writer? As a father of two, he feels the best gratification is watching his children enjoy the books he has written.

Extension Activities

- Invite students to use their mental cameras to "click" on school happenings. Later ask each student to illustrate and write a descriptive sentence about one memory on a sheet of drawing paper. Invite students to share their completed projects with their classmates; then compile the papers between two construction paper covers. Using construction paper scraps, decorate the front cover to resemble a camera. Place the finished booklet in your classroom library for further enjoyment.

- Place several hand mirrors and a colorful selection of water-soluble makeup sticks (such as Disguise Sticks) at a center. In small groups, have students "paint" their faces to resemble clowns. Invite each student to pantomime a clown act for his classmates.

Vocabulary

Chapter 1
lobby
arena
program
troupe
ringmaster

Chapter 2
platform
intermission
handbag
audience
wallet

Chapter 3
surrounded
apologize

Chapter 4
pickpocket
chalkboard
mustache
makeup

Chapter 5
Scotland
kilt

Chapter 6
aisle

Chapter 7
stall
handkerchief

Chapter 8
conductor
autograph

- Memory quizzes are loads of fun. Begin by displ ing a list of five items or a simple illustration. Ha students "click" on the display; then remove the display and begin the quiz. Students will enjoy recalling the items (in order) or details about the illustration. For an added challenge, feature more items or a more detailed illustration.

- It's intermission! Take a break and clown around with the tasty treats on page 35.

One Cool Clown!

Place a scoop of ice cream or yogurt on a luncheon-size paper plate. Squirt a ring of whipped topping around the scoop. Adorn the scoop with candy eyes and mouth, and a sugar-cone hat. Mmm! Mmm! Good!

One Cheesy Clown!

Place a scoop of cottage cheese on a luncheon-size paper plate. Add a lettuce bow tie, peach ears, grated-carrot hair, grape eyes, a cherry tomato nose, and a red-licorice mouth. Funny and yummy!

Creative Writing Activities

First have each student illustrate himself dressed as a clown. Then have the student write a paragraph which tells about his hilarious clown act! Mount the drawings and paragraphs atop 12" x 18" sheets of construction paper. Display the projects on a large circus tent cutout entitled "Now Appearing!"

Place four or five items in a brown grocery bag. Items might include a flashlight, a dog biscuit, a newspaper, and a candy wrapper; or a compass, a rope, a banana, a telephone book, and an envelope. Present the "clues" to your students; then have each write a short mystery adventure explaining how Cam and Eric solved a case using the clues.

Have each student design a large poster to announce the arrival of the circus. Each poster should include the following information: the location of the circus, the date and time of each circus performance, and the cost of admission. Have students use crayons or markers to decorate the posters as desired.

These easy-to-make, individual word banks are great writing motivators. Begin by having students brainstorm circus words. List these words on the chalkboard. Later transfer and duplicate student copies of the list, or have each student copy the list onto writing paper. Mount these lists on 9" x 12" sheets of yellow construction paper. To make a word bank, fold and cut a 3" x 9" piece of red construction paper as shown. Unfold; then match and staple the top corners of the cutout to the top corners of the yellow paper. (For added durability, tape the back of the project to join the yellow and red papers.) Slide the lower edge of the project under the red scalloped edge until it butts against the staples; then crease. Use markers or crayons to decorate the outside of the completed word bank. Students can peek "under the big top" for circus-writing motivation.

Critical Thinking Questions

1. Aunt Molly often covered her eyes during the circus acts. Do you think she enjoyed going to the circus? Why or why not?

2. Cam got her nickname because she can remember what she sees—just as if she'd taken snapshots. What do you think would be the best thing about having a photographic memory such as Cam's? The worst thing?

3. Why do you think some people are more forgetful than others?

4. Do you think Cam could have tracked down the pickpocketing clowns if they had been careful in removing their makeup? Why or why not?

5. What would you do if you saw someone take something that did not belong to him?

6. Why do you think Jack Wally was especially pleased that the pickpocketing clowns were caught?

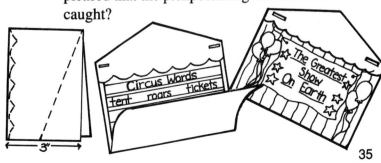

Click!

Read each clue.
Circle the matching word in the picture's border.
Then write the word on the line.

pmakeuplsieislobbylieinarenaostalltowndiwengazintermission

w
a
l
l
e
t
b
q
h
a
n
d
k
e
r
c
h
i
e
f
z
e
t
r
o
u
p
e
a
l
p
u
b
i
n

1. a large enclosed area

2. a narrow space for walking

3. a break during a show

4. a person's signature

5. a person who announces circus acts

6. a list of information about a show

7. a piece of cloth

8. to slow someone down

9. a group of performers

10. a thief

11. used to decorate the face

12. to say you are sorry

13. a waiting area

14. a money holder

1. _____

2. _____

3. _____

4. _____

5. _____

6. _____

7. _____

8. _____

9. _____

10. _____

11. _____

12. _____

13. _____

14. _____

b
i
o
a
u
t
o
g
r
a
p
h
s
l
d
i
n
f
o
a
i
s
l
e
e
o
a
p
o
l
o
g
i
z
e

leunareringmasterdnisoelwpickpocketahoes fnslprogramviens

Under The Big Top

Read the sentences in each group.
Use the code to color the circles.

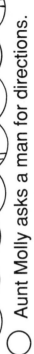

1. ○ Aunt Molly takes Cam and Eric to the circus.
   ○ Aunt Molly gives Cam a memory quiz.
   ○ Cam "clicks" on each page of the circus program.

2. ○ Aunt Molly loses her handbag.
   ○ Eric offers to buy ice cream with his money.
   ○ Aunt Molly discovers her wallet is missing.

3. ○ Cam asks a clown for help.
   ○ Cam goes in the ladies' room.
   ○ Cam and Eric discover more wallets are missing.

4. ○ Aunt Molly asks a man for directions.
   ○ The circus is over.
   ○ The guards capture the pickpockets.

5. ○ Aunt Molly identifies her wallet.
   ○ Jack Wally gives away free circus passes.
   ○ The pickpockets autograph circus programs.

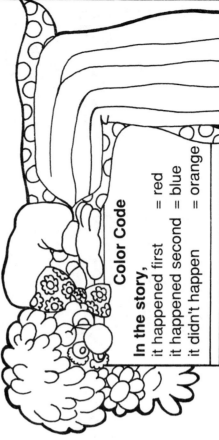

Color Code

In the story,
it happened first   = red
it happened second = blue
it didn't happen   = orange

Write your own sentences about the story.
Use the code to color the dots.

○ ○ ○

Clowning Around

Read the clues.
Cut out, match, and glue a hat to each clown.

1. colorful
   rubbery
   pops

2. pops
   salty
   yummy

3. cool
   yummy
   smooth

4. smooth
   colorful
   face

5. money
   holder
   valuable

6. ticket
   valuable
   fun

7. honest
   watchful
   helpful

8. dishonest
   watchful
   quick

9. flat
   smooth
   erasable

10. disguise
    fun
    clothing

wallet

police
officer

costume

ice
cream

balloon

popcorn

circus
pass

makeup

chalkboard

pickpocket

Arthur's Eyes

by Marc Brown

Wearing glasses is a big adjustment. When Arthur wears his new glasses to school, his friends tease him and call him four-eyes. None of his friends wear glasses. No one in his family wears glasses. Arthur decides to "lose" his glasses and suffers the embarrassment of an unexpected trip into the girls' bathroom. After talking with his teacher, who also wears glasses, Arthur puts his glasses on again and starts succeeding in school. His friend Francine is even envious enough to wear her own "movie star" glasses for the class picture.

The Author

With paper, pencils, and encouragement provided by his grandmother and uncle, and close supervision from his high school art teacher, Marc Brown was determined to become an artist. Although impressed by many artists, Mr. Brown feels that Maurice Sendak's wonderfully illustrated book, *Where The Wild Things Are,* determined the course of his life. Mr. Brown began his career illustrating textbooks. Later an editor encouraged him to write and illustrate children's books. Since that time, Mr. Brown has written and illustrated many books including the popular Arthur series. In his spare time Mr. Brown enjoys reading, gardening, and restoring antique houses. And he considers his red raspberry pie to be the best in the world!

Vocabulary

headaches	optometrist	problems
frames	handsome	laundry
principal	appeared	consider
surprised	concentrate	blind
photographer	polished	

Extension Activities

- Make diorama books to show favorite scenes from Arthur stories. Prior to beginning the project, have students bring in empty cereal boxes. Upon completing the book, have each student choose his favorite scene. Provide each student with a cereal box, colorful construction paper, glue, and markers to make a 3-D book.

   Reinforce the top and bottom of each cereal box with masking tape. Each student cuts the front of his box on three sides to make a book cover which opens. Have students decorate the outside of their boxes to represent books. Students then open their "books" and create three-dimensional displays inside. Complete the project by having the students write sentences on handwriting paper telling about their dioramas. Then glue the sentences to the inside covers. For a three-dimensional display, attach the boxes with straight pins to a bulletin board entitled "Arthur's Antics."

- If your students enjoyed *Arthur's Eyes*, they will be sure to enjoy the rest of this delightful series! When students have read each book in the Arthur series, they are eligible to become members of The Arthur Fan Club and Reading Association. To join, each eligible student must send $1.00 to:

   ARTHUR c/o Little, Brown and Company
   34 Beacon Street
   Boston, MA 02108

   Students will receive an official membership card and the most recent newsletter.

- Marc Brown has hidden his sons' names, Tucker and Tolon, in all but one of his Arthur books. Challenge your students to find Tucker's and Tolon's names (Tucker: pages 15 and 21, Tolon: page 21).

Creative Writing Activities

- Your young authors will delight in writing and illustrating their very own Arthur adventures! Provide students with white construction paper copies of the Arthur pattern on page 44, 4" x 18" strips of white drawing paper, crayons, and glue. Have students color the pattern as desired. Then have the students cut out the Arthur pattern along the bold cutting line and around Arthur's hands as shown. Have students accordion-fold the paper strip into five equal sections (approximately 3 1/2" per section) to create booklets.

   As a group, brainstorm a list of adventures such as Arthur's Ears, Arthur's Puppy Problems, or Arthur's Birthday Surprise. Then set your students loose to write and illustrate their new Arthur adventures. Allow time for willing students to share their stories with the class.

- After reading the story, tell students that they have received a letter from Arthur. As a group, read the letter below; then brainstorm a list of things that Arthur might do to remedy his situation. Then have students write letters to Arthur giving their advice. (Have students use Arthur's letter as a guide for letter format.)

                                                    (Date)

Dear students,
   Hi! My name is Arthur. I am having problems at school. I get headaches. I have trouble seeing the chalkboard, too. I am supposed to wear glasses, but my friends tease me. It makes me feel bad. What should I do?

                                        Sincerely,
                                        Arthur

"Mail" the letters to Arthur. Follow up this activi[ty] with another letter from Arthur thanking your students for their helpful advice.

- For each student, duplicate the eyeglasses patter[n] on page 44 onto the bottom of a full sheet of whi[te] construction paper. Have students fold their pape[r] on the dotted lines, then cut out the patterns alon[g] the bold cutting lines. Have students decorate the fronts of their glasses using markers, glitter, alun[i]num foil, and construction paper as desired. Ther[n] on the insides of their glasses, have students writ[e] stories explaining what their magical glasses help them to do. Display student work on a bulletin board entitled "Our Magical Glasses."

Critical Thinking Questions

1. Why do you think Arthur's friends teased him about his glasses?

2. How might the story have changed if they had been nice to him?

3. Why do you think it bothered Arthur that his friends were teasing him?

4. How would you have reacted to your friends if you were Arthur?

5. Which is more important to a friendship—a person's looks or his personality? Why?

6. Why do you think it made a difference to Arthu[r] that his teacher wore glasses too?

7. How do you think Arthur felt when he didn't ne[ed] Francine to help him with his boardwork any more? How do you think Francine felt? Why?

8. Why do you think Francine wanted to wear glasses in the school picture?

Name

Arthur's Search

Help Arthur find his glasses.
Read each question.
If the answer is **yes**, color the square **blue**.
If the answer is **no**, color the square **green**.

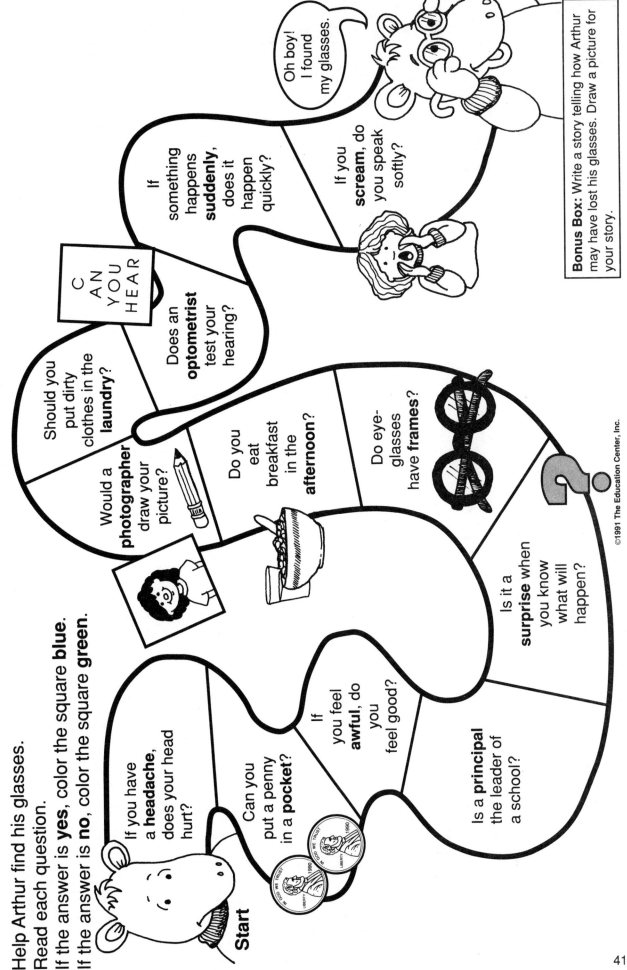

Start

If you have a **headache**, does your head hurt?

Can you put a penny in a **pocket**?

If you feel **awful**, do you feel good?

Is a **principal** the leader of a school?

Is it a **surprise** when you know what will happen?

Do eyeglasses have **frames**?

Do you eat breakfast in the **afternoon**?

Would a **photographer** draw your picture?

Should you put dirty clothes in the **laundry**?

CAN YOU HEAR

Does an **optometrist** test your hearing?

If something happens **suddenly**, does it happen quickly?

If you **scream**, do you speak softly?

Oh boy! I found my glasses.

Bonus Box: Write a story telling how Arthur may have lost his glasses. Draw a picture for your story.

©1991 The Education Center, Inc.

41

Arthur's Sequence Booklet

Read and draw a picture for each sentence.
Number the sentences in the order that they happened
in the story.

Arthur visits an optometrist and gets glasses. ◯	Arthur wears his glasses and does well in school. ◯
Arthur tries to lose his glasses. ◯	Arthur can't see well. ◯
Arthur's friends tease him. ◯	Arthur learns that his teacher wears glasses, too. ◯

Now cut on the dotted lines.
Stack the pages in order.
Staple to form a booklet.

Bonus Box: Make a cover for your booklet. Be sure to include the book title and author's name.

Name _____

Shooting Baskets

Read each sentence.
If the sentence is **true**, color the basketball **red**.
If the sentence is **false**, color the basketball **yellow**.

Arthur's friends said he looked handsome with his new glasses.

Arthur didn't like to be called four-eyes.

Bonus Box: On the back of this sheet, finish this story: Arthur dribbled quickly to the basket.... Draw a picture for your story.

Francine helped Arthur with his boardwork.

Arthur tried to lose his glasses.

Francine has real glasses.

Arthur's sister wears glasses.

Arthur hid his glasses in his desk.

Francine was in the boys' bathroom.

Arthur had headaches.

Arthur's teacher wears glasses, too.

Patterns and Award

Duplicate this award onto colorful construction paper. Use it to reward students who complete this book.

Use Arthur pattern with the first creative writing activity on page 40.

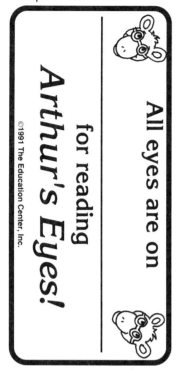

All eyes are on
Arthur's Eyes!
for reading

Use the eyeglasses pattern with the third creative writing activity on page 40.

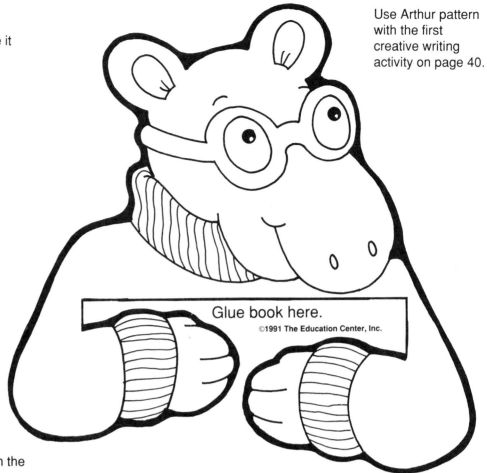

Glue book here.

Fold on the dotted line.

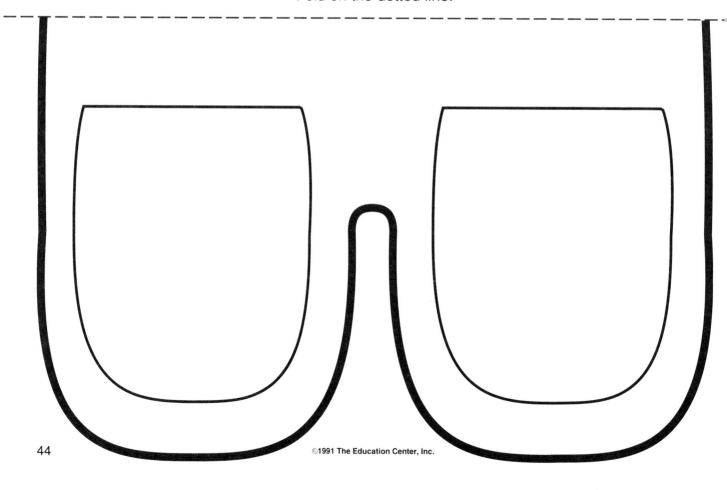

44

Horrible Harry In Room 2B

by Suzy Kline

Second grader Harry makes every day an adventure in Room 2B. His classmates call him Horrible Harry because he loves to do horrible things. He dangles his snake in front of Song Lee, launches an invasion of the stub people, and gets revenge by making Sidney say, "I love girls," twice! With Horrible Harry anything is possible! It's not easy being Harry's friend, but Doug knows that Harry isn't always horrible. Sometimes Harry can be pretty terrific. Just look out for knuckle noogies!

The Author

Suzy Kline has been an elementary schoolteacher in Torrington, Connecticut, for many years. Her classroom experiences serve as inspiration for her books. After reading *Horrible Harry In Room 2B,* you'll agree she knows what goes on in second grade. She says, "I get my ideas in the classroom; the children in the books aren't real, but the situations are." Beginning independent readers love the Horrible Harry series because they identify with him. Everyone knows a classroom character like Harry who is both horrible and lovable. Kline has also written a series of novels for slightly older readers about another character, Herbie Jones.

Vocabulary

Chapter 1

horrible	knuckles	canary
yogurt	tattoo	revenge
adventures	dangled	librarian

Chapter 2

invasion	assistant	enemy
permission	Frankenstein	skeleton
shivered	slithered	whispered

Chapter 3

cafeteria	Tyrannosaurus Rex	growled

Chapter 4

fertilize	mumbled	except

Chapter 5

aisle	drooled	aquarium
tropical	sardine	apricots

Extension Activities

- Horrible Harry showed his artistic talent with the creation of his stub people. Give your students the opportunity to design some stub people of their own. Ask students to bring in an assortment of odds and ends from home—yarn, fabric scraps, old buttons, pipe cleaners, and pencil or crayon stubs. Provide clay and a small paper plate for each child. Have each student make scary stub people using the clay and the plate for a base. Display creations and watch out for an invasion!

- Spotlight the characters in the story with "Who Am I?" bags. Give each child a brown, paper lunch bag. Have each student select a character from the story. Each child writes the name of his character on an index card and puts it in his bag. The student uses crayons and markers to decorate the outside of the bag with words or picture clues to his character. Students challenge each other to identify the characters by examining their bags. Students check the cards inside the bags to see if they are correct.

- Halloween was Horrible Harry's favorite holiday. Harry put a lot of effort into his horrible snake costume. Now Harry needs the help of your class to come up with a costume for next Halloween. Ask each student to design and illustrate a horrible Halloween costume for Harry. Display costume designs at Halloween with the title "How Horrible!"

- If your class enjoyed *Horrible Harry In Room 2B*, they may enjoy more of Harry's adventures in two other books by Suzy Kline, *Horrible Harry And The Green Slime* and *Horrible Harry And The Ant Invasion*. To culminate the series, have a Horrible Harry day. Make lime Jell-O for green slime and serve chocolate-covered raisins for "ants."

Critical Thinking Questions

1. Instead of delivering a cupcake to Mrs. Michaelsen, Harry and Doug eat it. Harry tells Doug they are doing her a favor. Do you agree or disagree with Harry's thinking? Why?

2. Horrible Harry and Sidney do not get along with each other. If you were Doug, what would you do to help Harry and Sidney become friends?

3. Harry declared that his stub people would bring "*doom* to the room." What do you think he meant? How do you think Harry felt when Miss Mackle called his stub people cute?

4. Do you think Harry lives up to his nickname? Why or why not?

5. If you could be one of the characters in the story, who would you be? Why?

6. Harry's idea helped Song Lee take part in the Thanksgiving play although she was very shy. Why do you think she was afraid to speak? How could you help someone overcome his or her shyness?

7. What might have happened if the bee had never landed on Doug's sandwich?

8. Do you think it would be difficult to be Harry's friend? Why or why not?

Creative Writing Activities

- Harry had a lot of creative ideas for writing. In h adventures at sea, "he met a mermaid, ate a sea turtle, and dug up a treasure." Ask students to pu their imaginations in high gear as they write abo their sea adventures with Harry. Have children include these vocabulary words: tattoo, mermaic sea turtle, Long John Silver, treasure. Continue t saga of The Adventures With Harry with creativ writing topics such as My Trip To Jupiter, An Amazing Ride Down The Amazon, On Safari W Harry, or Exploring Ancient Pyramids.

- The kids in Room 2B have invented a game call Knuckle Noogies. Have your students write a paragraph describing how to play this new game

- Mrs. Michaelsen, the librarian, is always on the lookout for books about snakes, slugs, dinosaurs and other "horrible" topics that Harry enjoys. Sh gives Harry a book on dinosaurs she knows he'll love. Harry informs her that she's "the best librar in the world." Give your school librarian a boost having students list three to five reasons why sh the best librarian in the world! Students can deli their lists on their next trip to the library.

- Harry is an expert on how to do horrible things. Have students work in pairs to brainstorm and th write a step-by-step paragraph telling how to do one of the following:
    how to give yourself a fake tattoo
    how to scare a girl
    how to pick a good library book
    how to capture a bee
    how to design a scary costume
    how to cook a sea turtle

Name _____

It's In The Bag

Doug shared his last chocolate chip cookie with Harry.
Read the meanings on the lunch bags below.
Look at the words on the cookies.
Cut out and paste the cookies to match the meanings.

a picture
on skin

a small
ocean fish

a
person who
helps

to take
by force

makes soil
richer

to
talk in a
low voice

to slide
along

a
warm
climate

to hurt
in return

to allow
someone
to do
something

©1991 The Education Center, Inc.

Bonus Box: Cut out 20 cookies from construction paper. Label ten cookies with words. Label the other ten cookies with matching definitions. Place all of the cookies in a lunch bag. Give it to a friend to make cookie pairs.

permit

assistant

mumble

tattoo

tropical

invade

slither

sardine

fertilizer

revenge

Invasion Of The Stub People

Meet the kids in Room 2B.
Read each phrase.
Think about who did it in the story.
Color the stub people by the code.

Color Code	
Harry	green
Doug	yellow
Sidney	orange
Song Lee	purple

 1. sat next to Harry in Room 2B

 2. brought cupcakes and fortune cookies for a birthday

 3. brought a book of bird stickers to school

 4. dangled a snake in front of Song Lee

 5. called Harry a canary

 6. gave knuckle noogies

 7. was Song Lee's partner on the field trip

 8. sat next to Miss Mackle on the bus

 9. wore a skull-and-crossbones tattoo

 10. was tricked into squeezing a slimy "slug"

 11. shared a chocolate chip cookie

 12. got sick at the first play practice

 13. was stung by a bee

 14. was Squanto in the class play

 15. made the stub people dance

Bonus Box: On the back, write three sentences that describe Miss Mackle.

Name _____

Here's One For Horrible Harry

Now that Harry has finished reading *Terrible Tyrannosaurus Rex*, he's looking for a new library book to enjoy. Be on the lookout for books about the horrible things Harry likes—snakes, slugs, sea turtles, spiders, and dinosaurs.

 Go to your school library.
 Pick a book you think Horrible Harry would like.
 Read the book.
 Complete the form.

Title _____

Author _____

Illustrator _____

Publisher _____

Copyright Date _____

This is the story of _____

_____

_____ .

Here is a picture of my favorite part.

_____

I think Horrible Harry will like this book because _____

_____

_____

_____ .

Book review prepared by _____

> **Bonus Box:** Design a bookmark for your book.

Keep The Lights Burning, Abbie

by Peter and Connie Roop

This story is based on events that occurred off the coast of Maine in January 1856. Young Abbie Burgess is asked by her father to keep the oil lamps burning in the lighthouse while he sails to Matinicus Island for supplies. A fierce, winter storm prevents him from returning, but Abbie proves that she is responsible and capable. She tends the lamps all night to insure that ships do not crash on dangerous rocks along the shore. Abbie's courage and caring are evident as she looks after her family during the month her father is gone.

Vocabulary

lighthouse	henhouse	patience
medicine	puffin	whitecaps
wicks	sailor	charity
sighed	ruffled	tower
dangerous	scraped	

The Authors

The authors were both born in 1951 and were married to each other in 1973. They have two children. Peter and Connie Roop were both classroom teachers. Connie taught junior high science and Pe[ter] taught grades one through four. Connie says her interest in children's books began while she was pursuing a master's degree in science teaching. Pet[er] was working on a master's degree in children's literature at the Center for the Study of Children's Literature at Simmons College in Boston. Connie began reading many of the books assigned to Pete[r] as a welcome change from science journals. She developed a fiction booklist to supplement her jun[ior] high science curriculum.

Their combined interests in travel and science ha[ve] led them to write nonfiction as well as historical books. Their first project together was a series of s[illy] joke and riddle books inspired by their "family tradition of word play." Two of their historical novels are *Keep The Lights Burning, Abbie* and *Buttons For General Washington*. Peter says they [are] interested in writing about "children who, like Abb[ie,] are 'footnotes in history.' "

Extension Activities

- Have students set sail for the library to research sailing vessels of the mid-1800s. Clipper ships, steamships, and schooners were once common when water transportation was the fastest way to travel. Students can expand their vocabularies by making charts, diagrams, and bookle[ts] of sailing ships and nautical terms.

- Display pictures of lighthouses and have students create lighthouse scenes. Explain that each lighthouse has a distinctive *day marker* pattern of brightly colored stripes or checks so it can be easily ident[i]fied by ships at sea. Supply Styrofoam cups, markers or crayons, clear plastic medicine cups, meat trays, and construction paper. To make a lighthouse, turn the Styrofoam cup upside down. Use markers or crayons to create a day marker pattern. Glue the clear, plastic cup to the bottom of the Styrofoam cup to form a beacon. Use a meat tray as the base of the scene and use construction paper to create the sho[re] and sea. Glue on pebbles for a rocky shore.

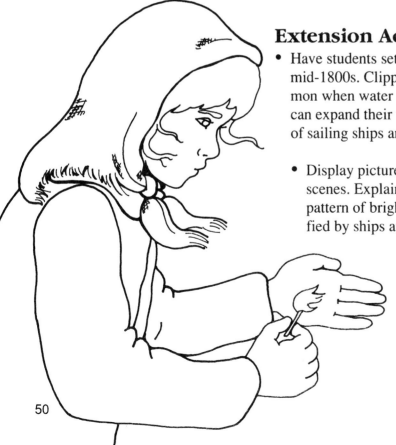

Abbie's courage and strength of character are an inspiration to other children. Have students design an award, commemorative stamp, or citation for Abbie Burgess. Display finished projects on a bulletin board that says "Shine On, Abbie!" Discuss young heroes of today.

Learning responsibility comes from being held responsible. Have students compare and contrast the responsibilities they have to those Abbie had. List responsibilities in two columns on the chalkboard. Have students survey parents to see what kinds of jobs they had as children. Students will get a new perspective on what is expected of others.

reative Writing Activities

In the 19th century, people often wrote about their feelings and observations in diaries and journals. Ask each child to write a diary entry for one of the stormy days from the point of view of Abbie, or Abbie's father, mother, or sister. Share the entries to present insights into the different characters.

Introduce the *simile* as a comparison of two things that includes the word *like* or *as*. Write this example on the chalkboard: "The beacon from the lighthouse was like a sailor's night-light." Allow students to try these simile starters:

The lighthouse was as tall as…
Being in a sailboat on a stormy sea is as scary as…
The cold seawater tasted like…
Welcoming Papa home was as wonderful as…

Have students illustrate their similes.

- Throughout her lifetime, Abbie continued to take care of lighthouses. In fact, her grave is marked by a miniature lighthouse. Have students write epitaphs or short descriptions of Abbie for her gravestone. Or have students describe Abbie's bravery for a historical marker on Matinicus Island.

- Put your junior investigative reporters on this interview assignment. Challenge pairs of students to brainstorm questions they would ask Abbie if she were being interviewed for their newsmagazine or TV news program. Record the questions on the board. Then have each child choose one question to answer with a three- to five-sentence paragraph.

Critical Thinking Questions

1. What do you think was Abbie's hardest job in keeping the lighthouse lamps burning?

2. Which qualities made Abbie an excellent lighthouse keeper?

3. Why did Abbie talk to her chickens? Tell of a time when having a pet made you feel better.

4. Pretend you are Mrs. Burgess. How would you show Abbie you are proud of her?

5. How do you know if someone is a responsible person? How do you show that you are responsible?

6. How do you think Abbie kept from being afraid during those four weeks? How do you keep yourself from being afraid?

7. If this story took place today, how would it be different? How would it be the same?

8. Why do you think the authors decided to tell this true story?

Hoist Your Sails!

Read each question.
If the answer is yes, shade the space on the lighthouse red.
If the answer is no, shade the space black.

1.
2.
3.
4.
5.
6.
7.
8.
9.
10.
11.
12.

1. Are **whitecaps** hats worn by sailors?

2. Can storms be **dangerous**?

3. Can a **lighthouse** be found at the airport?

4. Can a chicken **sigh**?

5. Is a **feather** heavy?

6. Should **sailors** know how to swim?

7. Will a lit **wick** glow?

8. Can a seagull **ruffle** its feathers?

9. Is a **puffin** a kind of cake?

10. Does a lighthouse have a **tower**?

11. Can **patience** change the weather?

12. Will you need **medicine** if you scrape your knee?

Bonus Box: Sailors give special names to the parts of the ship. *Bow, stern, starboard,* and *port* tell about the parts of the ship. Use a dictionary to find what these words mean. Write each word in a sentence on the back of this paper.

A Letter From Papa

Papa missed Abbie very much while he was gone for one month. In this letter, he wants to tell her how much he thought about her.

Finish the letter from Papa.

January 1856

My dear daughter Abbie,

   Thank you for being so responsible. It was a big responsibility
when you _____.
I was so proud that you _____.
It was not easy when you _____.
I knew that I could depend on you because _____
_____.

   Since you did such a wonderful job, I bought you the gift of a
_____ while I was away. This
gift reminded me of you because _____
_____.
I hope you will enjoy _____.

Love,
Papa

Bonus Box: If Papa gave Abbie a gift, she might share it with her sisters. On the back write three sentences that tell why you think Abbie would share.

Name_____

Hens In A Basket

Help match each chicken to its basket.
The first one is done for you.

Because Abbie wanted to feel better,    Papa could not sail home for four weeks.

Since Mama was ill,   Benjy could not help her light the lamps.

Because there was a winter storm for a month,   she talked to her chickens.

Since it was windy,   they steered away from the dangerous rocks.

Because her brother was fishing,   Papa sailed to Matinicus Island for medicine.

Since the ships could see the light   Abbie trimmed it.

Because there was ice on the windows,   there were many whitecaps on the waves.

Since the top of the wick was burnt,   she brought the chickens into the house.

Because she feared the henhouse would wash away,   Abbie scraped it off.

Since Papa had not returned with food   he hugged her tightly.

Because her sister was learning to read,   everyone was tired of eating eggs.

Since Papa was proud of how brave Abbie was,   Abbie helped her write her letters.

Bonus Box: Abbie's chickens are named Hope, Patience, and Charity. Find out what these names mean. Look in a dictionary. Write each definition on the back.

©1991 The Education Center, Inc.

Charlotte's Web
by E. B. White

A little girl named Fern saves the life of the runt of the pig litter. She names the piglet Wilbur and shares many happy hours with him and his barnyard buddies. When Wilbur hears that he's to be killed for Christmas, his friend Charlotte promises to save him. Charlotte is a very clever spider. With the help of Templeton the Rat, Charlotte weaves the words SOME PIG, TERRIFIC, and RADIANT into her web. Instead of becoming bacon, Wilbur becomes famous. He wins a special prize at the County Fair and is assured a long life on Mr. Zuckerman's farm. Charlotte's days, however, are numbered after she lays her eggs. Wilbur loses his loyal friend, but has the honor of knowing many generations of Charlotte's children.

The Author

E. B. White was born on July 11, 1899, in Mount Vernon, New York, and died in 1985. Although he was the youngest in a large family, he often felt lonely in a crowd and took to writing early. He wrote for the *New Yorker* and *Harper's* magazine for many years. In 1945, he published *Stuart Little*, his first children's book.

White wrote *Charlotte's Web* on his Maine farm. The idea for the story came to him one day on his way to feeding the pig. He explains, "…I began feeling sorry for the pig because, like most pigs, he was doomed to die." White started thinking of ways to save the pig. Over the next three years, he incorporated nature and the barn into the story. He watched goslings hatch and a big, gray spider spin its egg sac. He published *Charlotte's Web* in 1952. The book was named a Newbery Honor Book in 1953. White received several other awards for it over the years. In 1970, he received the Laura Ingalls Wilder Medal for "a lasting contribution to children's literature."

Vocabulary List

Chapter 1
   runt p. 1
   injustice p. 3
   blissful p. 7
Chapter 4
   hominy p. 26
   provender p. 26
   marmalade p. 26
Chapter 5
   objectionable p. 35
   salutations p. 35
   inheritance p. 39
   innocent p. 40
Chapter 6
   untenable p. 47
   lair p. 47
Chapter 7
   hysterics p. 51

Chapter 9
   spinnerets p. 58
   sedentary p. 61
   delectable p. 61
   vaguely p. 63
Chapter 10
   gullible p. 67
Chapter 11
   miracle p. 80
Chapter 12
   idiosyncrasy p. 86
Chapter 15
   monotonous p. 113
   versatile p. 116
Chapter 21
   desolation p. 165
Chapter 22
   aeronauts p. 179

Extension Activities

Wilbur was afraid he would be killed for bacon, ham, or pork chops. Have students cut out magazine pictures of products made from pigs. Have each child create a poster discouraging consumers from using pig products. Can your students make a case for Pig Power or Pigs Against Pork? Wilbur was awarded a "handsome bronze medal suitably engraved" at the County Fair. But he owed his fame to his special friends. Have each child design a medal for Charlotte or Templeton for saving Wilbur's life. Display the medals on a bulletin board. Create a friendship web by stapling lengths of black yarn in a web pattern. Add student-made medals and the title "True Friends Deserve Medals."

- Ask students to help Charlotte find just the perfect words to weave into her web. Have each child draw a spiderweb which shows five words that describe Wilbur. Have children share their webs and tell how the words describe Wilbur.

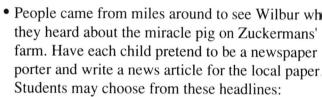

- Students can create models of Wilbur. Have each student cover a large oatmeal box with pink tissue paper. Use a section from a pink egg carton for a snout. Use two cardboard toilet paper tubes cut in half for legs. Add paper ears, eyes, and other features. Display pigs in a Pig Parade around the classroom.

Creative Writing Activities

- Fern named her pet pig Wilbur. She fed him from a bottle and took him for walks in a doll carriage. Discuss some of the things students learned from the book about caring for a pig. Have each student complete this story starter: I always wanted a pet pig. Pigs make great pets because…

- "The crickets felt it was their duty to warn everybody that summertime cannot last forever." Ask children what the crickets might be saying in their monotonous song. Have each child write a paragraph about what he misses the most when summer comes to an end.

- Wilbur ate an unusual variety of food slops. Read the descriptions of Wilbur's food on page 26. Have each child write a menu for Wilbur's dinner and share it with the class.

- People came from miles around to see Wilbur wh they heard about the miracle pig on Zuckermans' farm. Have each child pretend to be a newspaper porter and write a news article for the local paper Students may choose from these headlines:
  - Miracle Pig Discovered On Zuckerman Farn
  - Message In Web Points To Terrific Pig
  - Radiant Pig Does It Again

- Mrs. Zuckerman gave Wilbur a buttermilk bath to make him pure white and as smooth as silk. Have children imagine what Wilbur thought of the bath and write paragraphs from Wilbur's point of view

Critical Thinking Questions

1. Why was Mr. Arable going to shoot the runt of the litter? What would you have said to Mr. Arable to save Wilbur's life?

2. How could Fern have convinced her parents to let her keep Wilbu

3. Would you want a pig for a pet? Why or why not?

4. Why do you think all of the barnyard animals encouraged Wilbur to run away when he got out of his pen?

5. Do you think Wilbur's fame changed him? Why why not?

6. What might have happened if Charlotte had not come to Wilbur's rescue?

7. How do you think Fern felt about Wilbur's special medal?

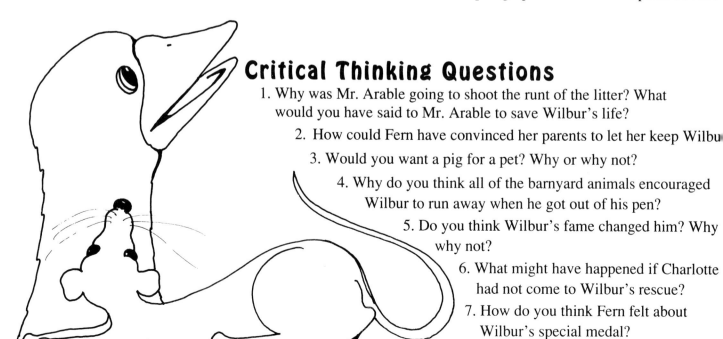

Name _____

Name _____

Charlotte's Web
Vocabulary

Wilbur's Web Words

Charlotte improved Wilbur's vocabulary by teaching him new words.
Read each meaning.
Look in the word bank.
Write Wilbur's matching vocabulary word on the line.

1. _____ the smallest pig in a litter

2. _____ easy to fool

3. _____ crying or laughing out of control

4. _____ greetings

5. _____ turning with ease from one thing to another

6. _____ passed on from parent to offspring

7. _____ sitting much of the time

8. _____ delicious, delightful

Word Bank

sedentary	hysterics	delectable	runt
	versatile	salutations	inheritance	gullible

Bonus Box: On the back, write each vocabulary word in a sentence about Wilbur.

©1991 The Education Center, Inc.

57

Name _____

Barnyard Buddies

Read the descriptive words and phrases in each picture frame.
Look at the word bank.
Write the character's name on the line.

selfish crafty lazy complaining	lays eggs stutters gabbles pipes up	clever loyal bloodthirsty patient

1. _____   2. _____   3. _____

speaks frankly experienced states the facts convinces rat to help	curious uses her imagination loves animals proud of her pig	radiant innocent humble fortunate

4. _____   5. _____   6. _____

Cut and paste the pictures below.
Glue a matching picture at each dot.

Bonus Box: On the back, write four words to describe Wilbur at the fair. Draw a snapshot of Wilbur with his special medal.

©1991 The Education Center, Inc.

Word Bank
Charlotte
Templeton
Goose
Sheep
Wilbur
Fern

Name _____

Wilbur's Riddle

What game is played with a little white ball that goes b-oink, b-oink?

Read each sentence.
Decide if it is a fact or an opinion.
Circle the letter in the correct column.
Write the letters in the blanks to find the answer to Wilbur's riddle.

		Fact	Opinion
1.	Fern spent too much time in the barn.	B	P
2.	It is unfair to kill the runt of the litter.	E	I
3.	Fern saved Wilbur's life once.	O	A
4.	Templeton was a crafty rat.	G	H
5.	Spiders are helpful because they eat bugs.	N	M
6.	Wilbur ate too much.	R	P
7.	Charlotte was doomed to die after laying her eggs.	G	T
8.	The sheep told Wilbur some bad news.	I	V
9.	Spiders are disgusting.	U	S
10.	People thought a miracle had happened on Zuckermans' farm.	T	W

__ __ __ '   __ __ __   __ __ __ __ !
8 10 9   6 2 7   1 3 5 4

Bonus Box: On the back, write five facts about spiders.

Name _____

Who Said It?

Read each quotation.
Decide who is speaking.
Write the character's name on the line.
Cross off the names below as you use them.

1. "The way to save Wilbur's life is to play a trick on Zuckerman. If I can fool a bug, I can surely fool a man. People are not as smart as bugs."

   _____

2. "It's the old pail trick, Wilbur. Don't fall for it, don't fall for it! He's trying to lure you back into captivity-ivity."

   _____

3. "A miracle has happened and a sign has occurred here on earth, right on our farm, and we have no ordinary pig."

   _____

4. "I prefer to spend my time eating, gnawing, spying, and hiding. I am a glutton but not a merrymaker."

   _____

5. "You're spending too much time in that barn—it isn't good for you to be alone so much."

   _____

6. "My best friends are in the barn cellar. It is a very sociable place. Not at all lonely."

   _____

7. "Well, I don't like to spread bad news, but they're fattening you up because they're going to kill you…"

   _____

8. "Children pay better attention than grownups. If Fern says that the animals in Zuckerman's barn talk, I'm quite ready to believe her. Perhaps if people talked less, animals would talk more."

   _____

9. "I know more about raising a litter of pigs than you do. A weakling makes trouble."

   _____

10. "Well, I've got a new friend, all right. But what a gamble friendship is!"

    _____

Fern	Mrs. Arable	Mr. Arable	Mr. Zuckerman
Charlotte	Sheep	Goose	Templeton
Wilbur	Dr. Dorian		

Name _____

A Spinner Of Tales

Spin a tale on Charlotte's web using one of these story starters:

Wilbur waited patiently for little spiders
   to emerge from Charlotte's egg sac.

After the fair, Wilbur was more famous than ever.
Mr. Zuckerman signed Wilbur up to star in a movie.

I always wanted a pet pig.

_____

_____

_____

_____

_____

_____

_____

_____

_____

_____

_____

_____

_____

Answer Key

Page 6
1. Fill a large pot with four quarts of water.
2. Add one tablespoon of salt to water and bring to a rapid boil.
3. Add pasta to boiling water and return to boil.
4. Cook uncovered for 12–16 minutes, stirring occasionally.
5. Test for doneness and drain pasta.
6. Serve with your favorite sauce.

1. Strega Nona put up a sign in the town square.
2. Strega Nona sang to the pasta pot.
3. Big Anthony sang to the pasta pot.
4. Big Anthony filled plates for all of the townspeople.
5. Big Anthony grabbed a cover and put it on the pot and sat on it.
6. Strega Nona gave Big Anthony a fork and told him to start eating.

Page 7

Read each question.
If the answer is yes, color the pot yellow.
If the answer is no, color the pot red.
Use a dictionary.

- Can a dog read the newspaper? Y
- Is a polo coin valuable? Y
- Can a pot of soup simmer? Y
- Can a lawn mower scurry? Y
- Would a nun live in a convent? Y
- Would you be telling the truth if you confess? Y
- Is there a cure for old age? R
- Would a barricade block traffic? Y
- Is a planet a loud noise? R
- Do clowns like applause? Y
- Is a punishment usually enjoyable? R
- Is stealing a crime? Y
- Could a priest say prayers? Y
- Could you drink a potion? Y
- Do most people hate compliments? R

Page 8

Strega Nona needed someone to help her.	The people did not believe Big Anthony's story.
Girls who wanted husbands went to Strega Nona.	Big Anthony had a chance to make the pot cook.
Big Anthony was angry.	Big Anthony did not blow three kisses.
Big Anthony was glad when Strega Nona went out of town.	Strega Nona made magic potions.
The pasta pot would not stop.	Strega Nona was getting old.
Big Anthony took a bow to the applause of the crowd.	They hoped God would stop the flood.
The men shouted, "String him up!"	They wanted to punish poor Big Anthony.
People barricaded the streets.	Big Anthony was a hero.
The priest and the sisters of the convent began to pray.	The punishment fit the crime.
Anthony had a tummy ache.	The pasta flood was coming.

Page 9

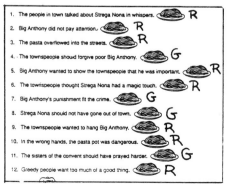

1. The people in town talked about Strega Nona in whispers. — R
2. Big Anthony did not pay attention. — R
3. The pasta overflowed into the streets. — R
4. The townspeople should forgive poor Big Anthony. — G
5. Big Anthony wanted to show the townspeople that he was important. — R
6. The townspeople thought Strega Nona had a magic touch. — R
7. Big Anthony's punishment fit the crime. — G
8. Strega Nona should not have gone out of town. — G
9. The townspeople wanted to hang Big Anthony. — R
10. In the wrong hands, the pasta pot was dangerous. — R
11. The sisters of the convent should have prayed harder. — G
12. Greedy people want too much of a good thing. — R

Page 12

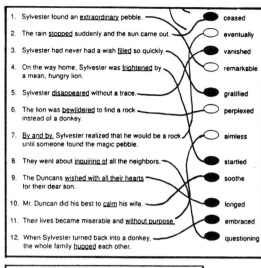

1. Sylvester found an extraordinary pebble. — remarkable
2. The rain stopped suddenly and the sun came out. — ceased
3. Sylvester had never had a wish filled so quickly. — gratified
4. On the way home, Sylvester was frightened by a mean, hungry lion. — startled
5. Sylvester disappeared without a trace. — vanished
6. The lion was bewildered to find a rock instead of a donkey. — perplexed
7. By and by, Sylvester realized that he would be a rock until someone found the magic pebble. — eventually
8. They went about inquiring of all the neighbors. — questioning
9. The Duncans wished with all their hearts for their dear son. — longed
10. Mr. Duncan did his best to calm his wife. — soothe
11. Their lives became miserable and without purpose. — aimless
12. When Sylvester turned back into a donkey, the whole family hugged each other. — embraced

Page 13

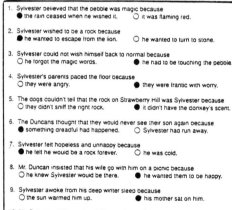

2 Sylvester wished it would stop raining.
1 Sylvester found a shiny red pebble.
3 Sylvester was startled by a hungry lion.
4 Sylvester said, "I wish I were a rock."

Meanwhile back at home,

1 Mr. and Mrs. Duncan paced the floor.
2 At dawn, the Duncans inquired of all the neighbors.
3 Sylvester's parents went to the police.
4 After a month, Sylvester's parents concluded that something dreadful must have happened.

One day in May,

1 Mr. and Mrs. Duncan went to Strawberry Hill for a picnic.
4 Sylvester wished to be himself again.
2 Mrs. Duncan sat down on a rock.
3 Mr. Duncan found the magic pebble and put it on the rock.

Page 14

1. Sylvester believed that the pebble was magic because
   ● the rain ceased when he wished it. ○ it was flaming red.
2. Sylvester wished to be a rock because
   ● he wanted to escape from the lion. ○ he wanted to turn to stone.
3. Sylvester could not wish himself back to normal because
   ○ he forgot the magic words. ● he had to be touching the pebble.
4. Sylvester's parents paced the floor because
   ○ they were angry. ● they were frantic with worry.
5. The dogs couldn't tell that the rock on Strawberry Hill was Sylvester because
   ○ they didn't sniff the right rock. ● it didn't have the donkey's scent.
6. The Duncans thought that they would never see their son again because
   ● something dreadful had happened. ○ Sylvester had run away.
7. Sylvester felt hopeless and unhappy because
   ● he felt he would be a rock forever. ○ he was cold.
8. Mr. Duncan insisted that his wife go with him on a picnic because
   ○ he knew Sylvester would be there. ● he wanted them to be happy.
9. Sylvester awoke from his deep winter sleep because
   ○ the sun warmed him up. ● his mother sat on him.
10. Mr. Duncan put the magic pebble in an iron safe because
    ● they couldn't wish for anything more. ○ it was dangerous.

Page 18

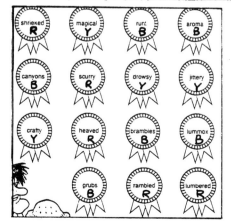

- shrieked R
- magical Y
- runt B
- aroma B
- canyons B
- scurry R
- drowsy Y
- jittery Y
- crafty Y
- heaved R
- brambles B
- lummox B
- grubs B
- rambled B
- lumbered R

Answer Key continued

Page 19

1. Bruce was a snaggy brute of a bear.
2. The bear ate a blueberry pie.
3. Bruce found himself nose to beak with a giant quail.
4. The huge boulder smashed pine trees and aspens.
5. Roxy put a magic spell on the blueberry pie.
6. Bruce ate beetles and grubs.
7. As Bruce slept he gradually grew smaller and smaller.
8. The bear exploded into great fits of laughter.
9. Roxy was out picking blueberries with her cat.
10. Bruce flopped down next to a tree to take a rest.
11. The tiny bear threw pebbles to scare the bugs.
12. Bruce smelled the aroma of blueberries and honey.
13. The cat and the bear ate out of the same bowl.
14. Roxy loved flowers, birds, and animals.
15. Klinker carried Bruce by the scruff of the neck.

Page 20

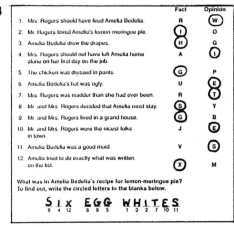

1. Bruce tumbled the rocks. They smashed the trees.
2. Bruce found a big boulder. He gave it a mighty heave.
3. The animals kept a sharp eye on Bruce. Just in case he gave them any trouble.
4. Bruce found a log. He found grubs and beetles under it.
5. Roxy and Klinker charged up the hill. "That rock could have smashed us to smithereens!"
6. The clever witch made a blueberry pie. She added a diminishing spell to it.
7. There was no sign of Bruce in the forest. But Roxy could hear him snoring around.
8. "Growl yourself!" the witch said to the bear. "You don't scare me."
9. The drowsy Bruce sat down next to a tree. He fell asleep by it.
10. Roxy and her cat made a plan. "We will show that bear," she said.
11. The witch grew fond of the tiny bear. She decided to keep him that way.
12. She picked out a pine stump. Then Roxy put the pie on it.
13. Klinker the cat liked the bear. They slept in the corner near the stove.
14. There were lots of rocks in Forevergreen Forest. Bruce could find great jumbles of them.
15. Laugh while you can, Mr. Bear," warned Roxy. "I will have the last laugh."

Page 21

1. Bruce tumbled rocks to scare the animals.
2. Bruce rolled a boulder that just missed Roxy.
3. The crafty witch hatched a plan.
4. Bruce gobbled up the magical blueberry pie.
5. As Bruce slept he grew smaller and smaller.
6. The forest animals chased the small bear.
7. The old witch took Bruce home to live with her.
8. Bruce flipped pebbles at the bugs in the garden.

Page 24

		Fact	Opinion
1.	Mrs. Rogers should have fired Amelia Bedelia.	R	W
2.	Mr. Rogers loved Amelia's lemon-meringue pie.	I	O
3.	Amelia Bedelia drew the drapes.	H	G
4.	Mrs. Rogers should not have left Amelia home alone on her first day on the job.	A	I
5.	The chicken was dressed in pants.	G	P
6.	Amelia Bedelia's hat was ugly.	U	E
7.	Mrs. Rogers was madder than she had ever been.	R	T
8.	Mr. and Mrs. Rogers decided that Amelia must stay.	S	Y
9.	Mr. and Mrs. Rogers lived in a grand house.	S	B
10.	Mr. and Mrs. Rogers were the nicest folks in town.	J	E
11.	Amelia Bedelia was a good maid.	V	S
12.	Amelia tried to do exactly what was written on the list.	X	M

What was in Amelia Bedelia's recipe for lemon-meringue pie?
To find out, write the circled letters in the blanks below.

S I X   E G G   W H I T E S
8 4 12   6 9 5   1 3 2 7 10 11

Page 25

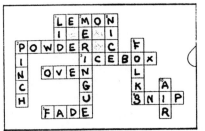

Page 27

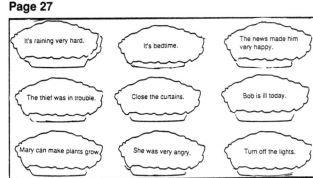

It's raining very hard.   It's bedtime.   The news made him very happy.

The thief was in trouble.   Close the curtains.   Bob is ill today.

Mary can make plants grow.   She was very angry.   Turn off the lights.

Page 30

1. figured
2. hollered
3. costume
4. practice
5. nursery
6. decided
7. neighbors
8. ruffled
9. audience
10. stomach
11. whisper
12. bounced

Page 31

1. Ms. Gumber
2. Mrs. Dissel
3. Mike
4. Freddy
5. Mr. Dissel
6. Ms. Matson
7. Mike
8. Ms. Matson
9. Freddy
10. Mrs. Dissel
11. Ellen
12. Ms. Gumber

Page 32

Answer to riddle: a mob of marsupials

Page 36

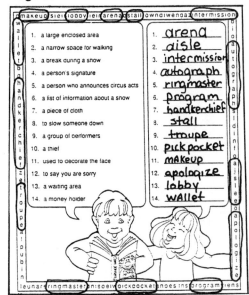

1. a large enclosed area
2. a narrow space for walking
3. a break during a show
4. a person's signature
5. a person who announces circus acts
6. a list of information about a show
7. a piece of cloth
8. to slow someone down
9. a group of performers
10. a thief
11. used to decorate the face
12. to say you are sorry
13. a waiting area
14. a money holder

1. arena
2. aisle
3. intermission
4. autograph
5. ringmaster
6. program
7. handkerchief
8. stall
9. troupe
10. pickpocket
11. makeup
12. apologize
13. lobby
14. wallet

Page 37

1. R Aunt Molly takes Cam and Eric to the circus.
   O Aunt Molly gives Cam a memory quiz.
   B Cam "clicks" on each page of the circus program.
2. O Aunt Molly loses her handbag.
   B Eric offers to buy ice cream with his money.
   R Aunt Molly discovers her wallet is missing.
3. B Cam asks a clown for help.
   O Cam goes in the ladies' room.
   R Cam and Eric discover more wallets are missing.
4. O Aunt Molly asks a man for directions.
   R The circus is over.
   B The guards capture the pickpockets.
5. R Aunt Molly identifies her wallet.
   B Jack Wally gives away free circus passes.
   O The pickpockets autograph circus programs.

Answer Key continued

Page 38

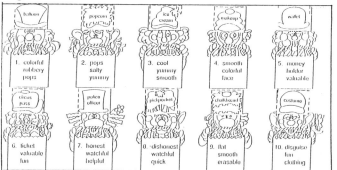

1. colorful
   robbery
   pops
2. pops
   salty
   yummy
3. cool
   yummy
   smooth
4. smooth
   colorful
   face
5. money
   holder
   valuable
6. ticket
   valuable
   fun
7. honest
   watchful
   helpful
8. dishonest
   watchful
   quick
9. flat
   smooth
   erasable
10. disguise
    fun
    clothing

Page 41

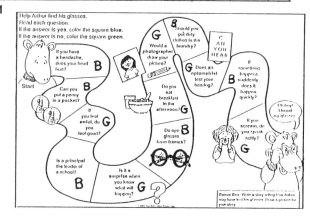

Page 43

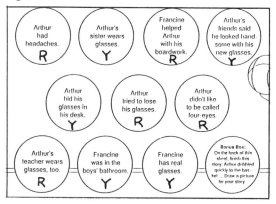

Arthur had headaches. **R**
Arthur's sister wears glasses. **Y**
Francine helped Arthur with his boardwork. **R**
Arthur's friends said he looked handsome with his new glasses. **Y**

Arthur hid his glasses in his desk. **Y**
Arthur tried to lose his glasses. **R**
Arthur didn't like to be called four-eyes. **R**

Arthur's teacher wears glasses, too. **R**
Francine was in the boys' bathroom. **Y**
Francine has real glasses. **Y**

Bonus Box: On the back of this sheet, finish this story. Arthur dribbled quickly to the basket ... Draw a picture for your story.

Page 47

tattoo — a picture on skin
sardine — a small ocean fish
assistant — a person who helps
invade — to take by force

fertilizer — makes soil richer
mumble — to talk in a low voice
slither — to slide along
tropical — a warm climate

revenge — to hurt in return
permit — to allow someone to do something

Page 48

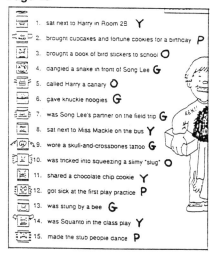

1. sat next to Harry in Room 2B **Y**
2. brought cupcakes and fortune cookies for a birthday **P**
3. brought a book of bird stickers to school **O**
4. dangled a snake in front of Song Lee **G**
5. called Harry a canary **O**
6. gave knuckle noogies **G**
7. was Song Lee's partner on the field trip **G**
8. sat next to Miss Mackle on the bus **Y**
9. wore a skull-and-crossbones tattoo **G**
10. was tricked into squeezing a slimy "slug" **O**
11. shared a chocolate chip cookie **Y**
12. got sick at the first play practice **P**
13. was stung by a bee **G**
14. was Squanto in the class play **Y**
15. made the stub people dance **P**

Page 52

1. No (black)
2. Yes (red)
3. No (black)
4. No (black)
5. No (black)
6. Yes (red)
7. Yes (red)
8. Yes (red)
9. No (black)
10. Yes (red)
11. No (black)
12. Yes (red)

Page 57

1. runt
2. gullible
3. hysterics
4. salutations
5. versatile
6. inheritance
7. sedentary
8. delectable

Page 58

1. Templeton
2. Goose
3. Charlotte
4. Sheep
5. Fern
6. Wilbur

Page 54

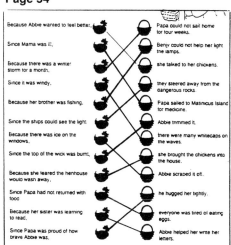

Page 59

Answer to riddle:
It's Pig Pong!

Page 60

1. Charlotte
2. Goose
3. Mr. Zuckerman
4. Templeton
5. Mrs. Arable
6. Fern
7. Sheep
8. Dr. Do
9. Mr. Ar
10. Wilbur